1000 Preserved Aircraft in Colour

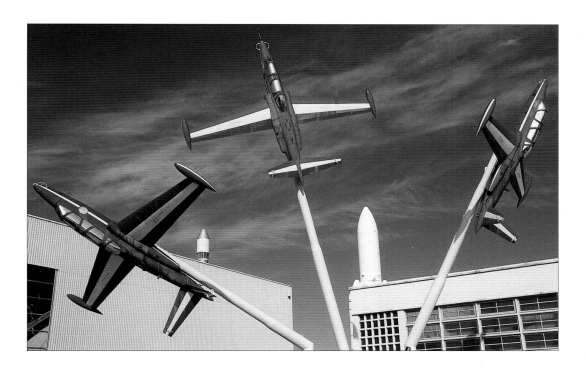

Gerry Manning

MIDLAND

An imprint of
Ian Allan Publishing

1000 Preserved Aircraft in Colour
© 2006 Gerry Manning

ISBN (10) 1 85780 229 2
ISBN (13) 978 1 85780 229 0

Published by Midland Publishing
4 Watling Drive, Hinckley, LE10 3EY, England
Tel: 01455 254 490   Fax: 01455 254 495
E-mail: midlandbooks@compuserve.com

Midland Publishing is an imprint of
Ian Allan Publishing Ltd

Worldwide distribution (except North America):
Midland Counties Publications
4 Watling Drive, Hinckley, LE10 3EY, England
Telephone: 01455 254 450   Fax: 01455 233 737
E-mail: midlandbooks@compuserve.com
www.midlandcountiessuperstore.com

North American trade distribution:
Specialty Press Publishers & Wholesalers Inc.
39966 Grand Avenue, North Branch, MN 55056
Tel: 651 277 1400   Fax: 651 277 1203
Toll free telephone: 800 895 4585
www.specialtypress.com

Design and concept
© 2006 Midland Publishing
Layout by Sue Bushell

Printed in England
by Ian Allan Printing Ltd
Riverdene Business Park, Molesey Road,
Hersham, Surrey, KT12 4RG

Visit the Ian Allan Publishing website at:
www.ianallanpublishing.com

Title page: Once flown by the French Air Force
display team the *Patrouille de France* the **Fouga
CM-170 Magister** was a two-seat trainer.
Pictured in the team's colours at the entrance to
the Musée de l'Air et de l'Espace at Paris-Le
Bourget, in June 2005, are three Magisters in a
'bomb-burst' display setting.

This page: Striking a dramatic pose at the
Canadian Warplane Heritage Museum at
Hamilton, Ontario, in August 2005, is Canadair-
built **Lockheed CF-104D Starfighter** 12641.
It is in the original polished metal fuselage, with
white wings, scheme that the type flew in
during the 1960s.

Introduction

The aim of the book is to show a range of the
many aircraft of all types that are preserved
worldwide. Some people may have their own
opinions about what is meant by 'preserved'.
I have defined this, for the purposes of this
work, as an aircraft that is either in a
museum, grounded such as a gate guard,
or one kept flying long after it would have
been normal to retire it. This covers the
many 'warbirds' and vintage aircraft to be
seen at airshows.

Since most museums tend to preserve
military aircraft rather than civil ones, due to
their history and availability, there is a bias
towards these, but many of the flying vintage
aircraft covered here are civil. There is today
a growing trend to preserve classic airliners
in flying condition, long may this continue.

The search for 'new' exhibits goes on
worldwide with discoveries in the most
unlikely locations every year of some
gem once thought to be lost.

I have tried to include as wide a
selection of types and locations as
possible from my travels around the
world, all the pictures having been
taken by myself.

Gerry Manning
Liverpool

Still in service after over forty years of operations with the USAF, the **Northrop T-38A Talon** still has a long life ahead of it before a replacement is selected. Nearly 1200 of the supersonic trainers have been built. 59-1600 is seen in October 1998 at the gate of the former Williams AFB, Arizona now Williams-Gateway.

The **Lockheed T2V-1 Seastar** (T-1A after 1962) was a deck-landing trainer operated by the US Navy. Service entry was 1957 and 150 aircraft were produced. The airframe was an adaptation of the original T-33. 144200 is pictured at the Pima County Museum, Tucson, Arizona in October 1998.

This **T-38A Talon** is pictured in August 1986 at Chanute AFB, Illinois, as No 1 in the colours of the USAF formation display team, *The Thunderbirds*. This museum has a number of types operated by the team and painted in their livery. The T-38 was operated before the current F-16.

Peru was an operator of the **Cessna T-37** but has replaced it in the pilot-training role with the Embraer T-27 Tucano at the Air Force Academy, Las Palmas, Lima. 61-474 is part of the Peruvian Air Force Museum collection at the base and is pictured in September 1997.

Above: First flown in 1954, the **Cessna T-37** is still the USAF's primary trainer, although it is in the process of being replaced by the T-6A Texan II. The Cessna is powered by a pair of 1,025 lbst Continental J69 turbojets. 55-4305 is displayed at the gate of Williams-Gateway, Arizona in October 1998.

Right: The **Cessna T-37** was exported to a number of countries under the Mutual Aid Program; the Royal Thai Air Force still operates the design. BF12-9/13 is on display at the RTAF Museum at Don Muang AFB Bangkok in November 1999. The dayglo is beginning to suffer under the harsh Thai sunshine.

Another South American country to fly the **Cessna T-37** is Colombia. It too has added the Tucano to the training role but still operates the T-37 at Palanquero. FAC 2112 is on display at the Colombian Air Force Museum at El Dorado, Bogotá in November 1992.

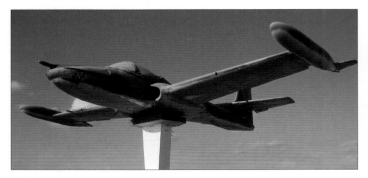

An armed version of the T-37 was developed by Cessna as the **A-37B Dragonfly**. It had powerplants of 2,850 lbst, eight wing hardpoints, a fixed machine gun and wingtip tanks, together with the facility for in-flight refuelling. This well-worn example, pictured in September 1997, is a gate guard at the Ecuadorian Air Force base at Manta where the type remains in service.

The **Cessna T-37** was evaluated by the US Army in 1958 for 'Project Long Arm'. This was to find a suitable fixed-wing jet for such roles as artillery spotting, ground attack and tactical reconnaissance. The aircraft was found to be ideal for the task but USAF opposition to the Army operating fixed-wing jets put paid to the project. 56-3465 is seen at the US Army Museum at Fort Rucker, Alabama in October 1981.

The most widely-produced western-built trainer is the **Lockheed T-33**. First flown in 1948, it was developed from the P-80 (later F-80) fighter. Power was provided by a 4,600 lbst Allison J33 jet, later increased to 5,400 lbst. 52-9734 is on display at the Air Power Park and Museum at Hampton, Virginia in May 1989.

Left: Designed as a military jet trainer to take pilots from elementary to 'wings' standard, the **Canadair CL-41 Tutor** first flew in January 1960. As well as its native Canadian operation it was sold to the Malaysian Air Force and also used for ground-attack operations. Pictured at the RCAF Memorial Museum at Trenton, Ontario is CL-41A 114015, in September 2005. The only current operator of the type is the CAF formation aerobatic team *The Snowbirds,* officially known as 431 Air Demonstration Squadron.

Below: The Bolivian Air Force still operates an armed version of the **Lockheed T-33** as its front-line fighter. Preserved inside Base Aerea *General Walter Arze* El Alto Airport, La Paz in November 1992, is Canadian-built T-33AN FAB 602.

Being the most widely-produced jet trainer has meant that the **Lockheed T-33** has served, and in some cases continues to serve, in many locations around the world. As they are withdrawn some examples are preserved. FAC 2018 is at the gate of Base Aereo Luis F Gomez Nina at Apiay, Colombia in September 1997.

Left: A Canadian-built version of the Northrop F-5 was chosen, in 1965, to replace the Sabre. This was designated **Canadair CF-5** (later CF-116). Power came from a pair of Orenda-built GE J85 turbojets. The type was retired from service during the 1990s due to defence cuts. Pictured at the RCAF Museum at Trenton, in September 2005, is 116721. It is in the special colour scheme worn by display aircraft from 419 Squadron.

Below: Many air forces around the world operated the **Lockheed T-33**. Pictured at the Republic of Singapore Air Force Museum at Paya Lebar, in February 2003, is T-33A 364 ex-51-6956.

Pictured at the Military Museum of China, Beijing, in December 1987, is this Nationalist Chinese **Lockheed T-33A** T-33024/52-9971. It is one of a number of western designs exhibited following either capture or pilot defection.

The US Air National Guard flew the **F-100 Super Sabre** for 21 years before phasing out the type in 1979. Seen up a pole at Kirtland AFB, New Mexico in October 1984, is F-100A 53-1532. This is the home base of the 188th Fighter Squadron, which was the first Air National Guard unit to operate the design when it converted from F-80s in 1958.

Above: In the early 1970s the USAF held a competition for a new lightweight fighter between the General Dynamics YF-16 and the **Northrop YF-17**. The winner was the YF-16. However the YF-17 was not finished as it was then developed by McDonnell Douglas into the F/A-18 Hornet. Pictured at the Western Museum of Flight, Hawthorne, California in October 2001 is YF-17A 72-1569.

Right: The **North American F-100 Super Sabre** was the first fighter in operational service to achieve supersonic speed in level flight. First flown in 1953, it served the USAF as an interceptor and later as a fighter-bomber. France was one of several countries to operate the F-100. F-100D 54-2165 wears the markings of Escadre 2/11, in May 1987, and is part of the Imperial War Museum collection at Duxford. It has since been repainted in USAF markings.

The 152nd Fighter Squadron of the Arizona ANG has this **F-100D Super Sabre** 56-3055 on display outside its Tucson headquarters. It is pictured in September 1988.

Toledo Express Airport is the home base of the 112th Fighter Squadron Ohio ANG. This unit converted to the **F-100 Super Sabre** from F-84Fs in 1970 and flew them until they were replaced by A-7Ds in 1979. F-100D 55-2855 is at the unit's gate in July 1986.

Showing off the wonderful colour schemes the USAF used to sport is this **F-100D Super Sabre**. 56-3288 is pictured, in October 2001, at the McClellan Aviation Museum, California.

One of the most famous users of the **F-100 Super Sabre** was the USAF formation display team *The Thunderbirds*. F-100D 55-3754 is marked as 'Six' at the USAF Museum at Wright-Patterson AFB, Dayton, Ohio in July 1986.

Left: Second of the 'Century Series' was the **McDonnell F-101 Voodoo**. Its original role was as a long-range escort fighter for the bombers of Strategic Air Command. First flown in 1954 it entered service with Tactical Air Command after SAC had revised its needs. F-101B 56-0235 is on display at the Yankee Air Museum, Willow Run, Michigan, in June 1990.

Below: The **F-101 Voodoo** was used as a photographic reconnaissance platform in two variants. The RF-101B was a conversion of the F-101B two-seat long-range fighter, and was operated by one unit only. This was the 192nd Tactical Reconnaissance Squadron Nevada ANG, which flew it from 1971 to 1975 when replacement came in the form of the RF-4C Phantom. RF-101B 59-0483 is displayed outside the unit's base at Reno-Cannon in September 1988.

The production reconnaissance Voodoo was the single-seat RF-101A or C model. The definitive variant had a re-shaped nose for the camera installations. Painted in Taiwanese markings, one of the few nations to operate the type, is 41518/56-0229 – an **RF-101C**. It is on display at the Museum of Aviation at Warner Robins AFB, Georgia in April 1994.

Canada was one of the nations to fly Voodoos. Designated CF-101 they flew as long-range interceptors. **CF-101B** 101057 is displayed in spectacular markings at the gate of the Canadian Armed Forces' base at Comox, British Columbia in May 2000.

The **Convair F-102 Delta Dagger** was a single-seat, all-weather fighter-interceptor. First flown in 1953, it entered service with the USAF two years later. The last users were ANG fighter units. Photographed in September 1988, the 152nd Fighter Squadron Arizona ANG has F-102A 56-1134 on display at its Tucson base.

Above: Despite its high performance and radical design, for the time, the **Lockheed F-104** did not have a long service life with the USAF. F-104C 56-0934 is seen at George AFB, California in October 1979.

Below: Following the closure of George AFB, **F-104C Starfighter** 56-0934 moved north to the Museum of Flight run by Boeing at Boeing Field, Seattle, Washington. It is pictured, in May 2000, painted as N820NA/NASA 820 in the livery of the National Aeronautics and Space Administration. NASA flew Starfighters from the Dryden Flight Research Facility at Edwards AFB California. At that location can be found the real NASA 820 (56-0790), an F-104A.

The **Convair F-102** was the first delta-wing aircraft in service and the first fighter to be built without guns; its weapon load being all missiles, both guided and unguided. F-102A 56-1114 is at the gate of Luke AFB, Arizona in October 1979.

For combat training the USAF purchased 63 **TF-102A Delta Dagger** two-seat aircraft. The type had side-by-side seating fitted in a widened nose section. 54-1351 was the first of these and is seen at Chanute AFB, Illinois in August 1986.

The most recognisable of the 'Century Series Fighters' has to be the **Lockheed F-104 Starfighter**. It was dubbed 'the missile with a man in it', first flown in 1954 it passed Mach 2 the following year. Japan was one of the early customers for the type with a 1960 order for the local-built F-104J. 76-8688 is pictured as a gate guard at Naha AFB, Okinawa in October 2004.

Left: Canada licence-built the Starfighter as the **Canadair CF-104**. This example, 104763, is in the special markings of 417 Operational Training Squadron at the Reynolds Aviation Museum, Wetaskiwin, Alberta in September 2005.

Below: The Greek Air Force received Starfighters second hand from a number of European operators. **F-104G** 6695 is an ex-Dutch machine and is displayed at the Hellenic War Museum in Athens in June 1993.

In 1963 three Starfighters were modified by the installation of a 6,000 lb-thrust Rocketdyne AR-2 rocket motor fitted in addition to the General Electric J79 turbojet. This extra power pushed the aircraft to altitudes of 130,000ft. Their role was to train test pilots and potential astronauts at the USAF Test Pilots School at Edwards AFB. **NF-104A Starfighter** 56-0760 is pictured there, in October 1979. Note the location of the rocket in the base of the fin.

The US Navy used the **General Dynamics F-16** for aggressor training in its Fighter Weapons School, better known as *Top Gun*. F-16N 163271 is pictured, in October 2001, at the Pacific Coast Air Museum, Santa Rosa, California. The F-16N variant has no capability as a fighter as it lacks guns, missiles and radar. This lightweight aircraft does however have excellent manoeuvrability.

Above: The largest user of the Starfighter was the Federal German Republic which purchased a total of 914, both single- and two-seaters for the Luftwaffe and Navy. The type suffered high losses and was dubbed 'The Widow Maker' by the German press. DB+127 (later 20+02) is a Lockheed-built **F-104G/ZELL**. This version was a 'Zero Length Launch' aircraft powered by a ramp-mounted Rocketdyne motor that would take the aircraft to safe flying speed before being dropped. It is seen in May 2004 at the Luftwaffe Museum at Gatow, Berlin.

Right: Designed as a supersonic tactical fighter, the **Republic F-105 Thunderchief** first flew in 1955 and entered service four years later. The two-seat trainer version of the Thunderchief was the F-105F, which first flew in 1963 and entered service later that year. 63-8287 has the 'RU' tail code of the 355th TFW, a unit that operated over Vietnam until the end of 1970. It is at Chanute AFB, Illinois in August 1986.

The F-105 was designed to carry both conventional and nuclear weapons. It is fitting that the Sandia Atomic Museum at Albuquerque, New Mexico, should display one. **F-105D Thunderchief** 61-0107 is seen, in October 1984, mounted on a pole.

Above: The purpose of the 'Wild Weasel' in the USAF is to attack enemy ground-based radar sites. The first type to carry out the role was the F-100, but it is the **F-105G Thunderchief** that brought fame to this dangerous task. 62-4427 is at the Pima County Museum, Arizona in September 1988.

Right: The 'D' model of the F-105 was the definitive service variant and had added all-weather systems. Power was provided by a single Pratt & Whitney J75 turbojet of 24,500 lb thrust with afterburner. **F-105D Thunderchief** 61-0165 is in tactical camouflage at the gate of George AFB, California in October 1979.

Two-seat Delta Darts were designated **F-106B**. This combat trainer in tandem-seating configuration had full mission capability. 57-2523 is pictured displayed, in May 1989, at Andrews AFB, Washington DC.

Above: The **Convair F-106 Delta Dart** was one of the most elegant air-defence fighters. An extensive development of the F-102, it was in fact a complete weapons system. First flown in 1956, it remained in service with the USAF until 1988. F-106A 59-0146 is pictured as part of the 144th Fighter Interceptor Wing Collection at Fresno Air Terminal in August 1986.

Right: Last of the line of 'Century Series Fighters' was the **North American F-107**. Its role was to have been that of a tactical fighter-bomber. Its first flight was in 1956 and it had a futuristic look with the air intake above the cockpit. Three examples were flown before it was cancelled in favour of the F-105 in 1957. YF-107A 55-5118, the first prototype, is displayed, in October 1984, at the Pima County Museum.

America's first operational jet aircraft was the **Lockheed P-80**. First flown in 1944, deliveries began to the US Army Air Force later that year. It was re-designated F-80 in 1948 with the creation of the USAF. F-80C 49-0710 is seen displayed, in October 1984, with a range of missiles at Alamogordo, New Mexico.

The 144th FBS of the Alaskan ANG flew F-80s for two years from 1953 until they were replaced by F-86 Sabres. **F-80C** 49-1849 is on display in May 2000 at Kulis ANG Base, Anchorage in a high-visibility scheme.

Following the withdrawal of the F-80 from ANG units, a number of South American air forces obtained these aircraft under the Military Assistance Programme. Colombia was one such air arm, and **F-80C** FAC 2061 is on show at its air force museum at Bogotá in November 1992.

Ecuador was another of the South American air arms to receive the **Lockheed F-80**. FT-714 is pictured in September 1997, mounted on a pole outside the officers' mess at Base Aerea Taura.

Above left: The Thunderjet, Thunderstreak and Thunderflash, all had the designation F-84. The first of these, the Thunderjet, was designed by Republic as a jet fighter replacement for the P-47 Thunderbolt and was a straight-wing subsonic airframe powered by a General Electric J35 turbojet. **F-84C** 47-1433, the second production model, is seen in October 1998 wearing the colourful markings of the period at the Pima County Museum, Arizona.

Above right: The 'G' model of the Thunderjet had a more powerful engine and an autopilot. It was exported to a number of American allies. **Republic F-84G** 878/1231 is on display, in November 1999, at the Royal Thai Air Force Museum in Bangkok.

Left: NATO air forces flew the **F-84G Thunderjet**. K171/DU-24 is pictured at Deelen, in June 1973, but is now preserved at the Royal Dutch Air Force Museum at Soesterberg.

Left: A swept-wing variant of the F-84 was produced by Republic. Power for this was provided by a single Wright J65 Sapphire of 7,220 lbst. This model was known as the **F-84F Thunderstreak**. As well as the USAF, many European air arms operated the type. BF+105 is an ex-Luftwaffe machine and is seen, in May 1983, on display at the Flugausstellung L&P Junior at Hermeskeil in Germany.

Below left: Part of the Luke AFB Heritage Park collection in Arizona is this **F-84F Thunderstreak** '52-6779'. It is pictured, in October 1979, in the markings of *The Thunderbirds* team, which was formed at the base in 1953. Its true identity is 52-6782.

Below right: **F-84F Thunderstreak** 51-9433 is pictured, in October 2001, at the Castle Museum, California.

Above left: A few **F-84F Thunderstreaks** have found their way onto the US civil aircraft register for use by private owners. N84JW is seen on the ramp at Mojave, California in October 1979.

Above right: The glorious markings of the 1950s put today's grey-on-grey into the shade. 52-6701 **F-84F Thunderstreak** is on show, in April 1994, at Warner Robins AFB, Georgia.

Right: Belgium was another of the NATO users of the **F-84F Thunderstreak**. FU-30 is seen in, June 1983, at the Royal Army Museum in Brussels.

FICON was a programme for a 'Fighter Conveyor', where an F-84 was carried below a Convair B-36 bomber to give fighter protection at locations beyond the range of conventional operations. The aircraft had a retractable hook in the nose and anhedral on the tailplane to clear the bomb bay of the B-36. It was designated **RF-84K**. 52-7265 is pictured, in October 1984, at the Fighter Jets and Air Racing Museum at Chino, California.

Above: In 1952 Republic developed the third variant of the F-84. This was the reconnaissance version with cameras in the nose. This led to the air intakes being repositioned in the wing roots. It was designated **RF-84F Thunderflash**. 52-7244 is seen at Warner Robins AFB in April 1994.

Right: Two F-84s were converted from turbojet to turboprop power with the fitting of a 5,850shp XT40-A-1 powerplant. It had a supersonic propeller and first flew in 1955 as a joint USAF/USN project. 51-17059, designated **XF-84H**, is on display at Bakersfield Airport, California in October 1984. It has since moved to a new location at Edwards AFB.

The price of the **Aero L-39 Albatros** has proved to be popular with American private pilots and they fly in many parts of the country. N454WF carries bogus, but attractive, US Navy livery at Lakeland, Florida in April 2005.

Above: The **Aero L-39 Albatros** evolved from the earlier L-29 Delfin and since entering service with the Czechoslovakian Air Force in 1974 went on to fulfil the advanced training role in Russia, most of its satellites, and other countries around the world. L-39ZO 143 is a retired DDR example pictured in May 2004 at the Luftfahrttechnischer Museumverein at Rothenburg. This variant is the weapons trainer with reinforced wings and four hardpoints for weapons stores under each wing.

Left: The **North American F-86 Sabre** was without doubt the most widely-used free-world fighter. It entered service with the USAF in 1949 and continued in military markings until the early 1990s when the Bolivian Air Force disposed of its last three. A considerable number can be found flying in private hands. F-86A G-SABR/48-0178 is seen at an airshow at RAF Fairford in July 1997.

The 'F' model Sabre featured a new wing leading edge design. This increased manoeuvrability at high altitude. Many combats in the Korean War were flown at 50,000ft. **F-86F Sabre** 1A36 is pictured, in November 1992, at the Venezuelan Air Force Museum at Maracay.

Above: Seen at Kulis ANG base, Anchorage, Alaska, in May 2000, is **F-86A Sabre** 49-1195. It is painted to represent F-86E 51-2807 of the 144th FIS Alaska ANG in which Captain Richard A Otto died in an accident in February 1957. It is dedicated to his memory.

Left: Nicknamed the 'Sabre Dog' the **F-86D** was an all-weather interceptor with the nose re-configured for the radar set. Its GE J47 engine produced 7,650 lb thrust and incorporated an afterburner. 51-6171 is one supplied to the Greek Air Force under the Mutual Defence Aid Programme. It is seen displayed at the Hellenic War Museum in Athens in June 1993.

On show at the Military Museum of China in Beijing, in December 1987, is **F-86F Sabre** F-86272/52-4441. This Chinese Nationalist Air Force example is one of a number of types either captured or obtained through pilot defection.

Portugal received its Sabres from ex-Luftwaffe stocks and used them in the 1960s in colonial wars as ground-attack aircraft. **F-86F** 5316 was presented to the Royal Army Museum in Brussels where it is seen exhibited in June 1983.

The Japanese Air Self Defence Force's first operational **F-86F Sabre** wing was established at Hamamatsu in 1956 with Mitsubishi-assembled aircraft. Pictured at Komaki air base, Nagoya, in October 2004, is 82-7778 on gate guard duties.

The final production version of the Sabre was the 'H' model. It was both longer and wider and was powered by a GE J73 powerplant of 9,300 lbst. **F-86H Sabre** 53-1304 is seen, in October 1984, wearing a rare camouflage scheme for the type at March AFB Museum, California.

The 'K' version of the Sabre was developed as an all-weather radar-equipped fighter for NATO. Production was by North American and Fiat in Italy. Pictured, in June 1973, is **F-86K** Q305 of the Dutch Air Force at Deelen. This Italian-built machine is now in the air force museum at Soesterberg.

Nearly 1,000 F-86Ds were converted to F-86L standard. This included new radar and the longer wing of the 'H' model. The variant was exported to only one nation. **F-86L Sabre** 1215/53-0681 is in the colours of 12 Squadron Royal Thai Air Force at its museum at Bangkok in November 1999.

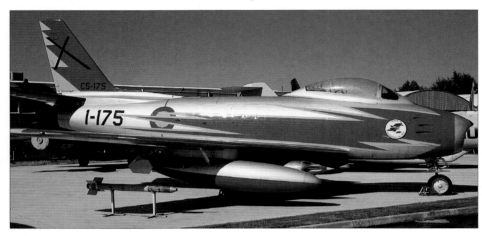

Left: 1955 saw the first of 207 **F-86F Sabres** being delivered to the Spanish Air Force (Ejercito del Aire). They remained in service until the end of 1974. Pictured in September 2002 at the Museo del Aire, Madrid is C.5-175. It is in the livery of the *Ascuas* aerobatic team who operated the type from the late 1950s into the early years of the following decade.

Right: Many **F-86Ls** flew with units of the Air National Guard. 52-3651 was once operated by the 128th FIS Georgia ANG at Dobbins AFB. It is pictured, in April 1994, displayed outside the administration building at Lewis B Wilson Airport, Macon, Georgia.

Below: When in 1948 Canada selected the Sabre as its next fighter, it was decided to build it in the country with Canadair as the manufacturing company, and with the designation **CL-13**. Sabre 5 23047 is displayed at Oshawa Airport, Ontario in July 1986.

During its operational life with the USAF the Sabre sported some of the best colour schemes ever seen on fighters. **F-86L Sabre** 51-3064 is at the Air Power Park, Hampton, Virginia in May 1989.

Above left: The **Canadair CL-13 Sabre** 5 and 6 differed from equivalent American-built airframes by having an Avro Orenda powerplant. Pictured on display at the RCAF Memorial Museum at Trenton, Ontario, in September 2005, is Sabre 5 23257 in the flamboyant markings of *The Golden Hawks* aerobatic team. They were formed at the end of 1959 and operated until 1963, during which time they flew over 300 displays.

Above right: The majority of the production of the **Canadair CL-13 Sabre 4** was delivered to the RAF under the Mutual Aid programme. They were replaced in the mid 1950s by the Hawker Hunter, the Sabres being transferred to Italy and Yugoslavia. Pictured, in September 2004, at the Italian Air Force base at Grazzanise on gate guard duties is Sabre 4 MM19523.

Right: West Germany was a recipient of ex-Royal Canadian Air Force Sabre 5 and 6s. **CL-13 Sabre 6** D-9539 is one of several models of Sabre in the Luftwaffe Museum at Gatow, Berlin, in May 2004.

Above left: Designed by Northrop the **F-89 Scorpion** was a twin-engined, twin-seat, all-weather radar-equipped fighter. First flown in 1948, more than 1,000 were constructed for the sole customer, the USAF/ANG. F-89J 53-2453 is displayed, in May 2000, at Elmendorf AFB, Anchorage, Alaska.

Above right: Only two airframes of the **Republic F-91** interceptor were built. First flown in 1949 it was powered by a J47 turbojet together with an extra XLR11 rocket motor. XF-91 46-680 is at the USAF Museum at Dayton, Ohio in July 1986.

Right: Lockheed's **F-94 Starfire** can trace its roots back to the F-80. The F-94 was a much larger machine, a two-seat radar-equipped all-weather fighter. F-94C 51-5623 is at the Pima County Museum, Arizona in October 1998.

Above: Despite its fighter role, the **F-94 Starfire** was not fitted with a gun. Its armament was 24 unguided rockets in the nose and 12 in each of two wing pods. F-94C 51-13575 is pictured in July 1986 at the New England Air Museum, Windsor Locks, Connecticut.

Below: McDonnell followed the Phantom I with the Banshee. The basic layout was similar but the whole airframe was much larger and the powerplants gave nearly twice the thrust. **F2H-2 Banshee** 124988 of the US Marine Corps is on show at the gate at El Toro, California in September 1988.

The first jet to land on a US Navy carrier was the **McDonnell Phantom I**. Power was provided by a pair of Westinghouse J30 turbojets of just 1,600 lbst. As a carrier-borne fighter it had a short career, soon being replaced by more advanced types. FH-1 Phantom 111793 is pictured, in April 1994, at the US Navy Museum at Pensacola, Florida.

Above: The first jet fighter from the North American company was the **FJ-1 Fury** for the US Navy. It was a single-seat, carrier-borne, straight-wing, subsonic fighter. Only one squadron was ever equipped with the type but it had the distinction of being the first jet fighter to go to sea in an operational role. FJ-1 Fury 120351 is at the US Navy Museum at Pensacola, Florida in April 1994.

Left: As well as US Navy operations the Fury found service with the US Marine Corps. In the livery of VFM-333, **FJ-3 Fury** 136022 is seen at the gate of El Toro, California in September 1988.

One of the best locations for an aircraft museum has to be that of the retired aircraft carrier USS *Intrepid* (CV-11) docked in New York Harbor. In the colourful navy squadron markings of VF-191 is **FJ-3 Fury** 135868, preserved on the flightdeck in May 1989.

The name Fury was used once again by North American for the naval version of the F-86. Three prototypes were ordered by the US Navy in 1951. For carrier deck operations many changes were needed, not least folding wings. **FJ-3 Fury** 135867 is part of the Fighter Jets Collection at Chino, California. It is pictured in September 1988, with its wings folded.

The **McDonnell Douglas F-4 Phantom II** can claim to be one of the most versatile warplanes ever built. With more than 5,000 produced it is still in service with most of the air forces that have operated it. Originally intended as an all-weather fleet defence fighter for the US Navy, 151497 is an F-4B, the first real service version, preserved at the Pima County Museum in October 1998.

The USAF Flight Demonstration Team, better known as *The Thunderbirds*, operated the **F-4 Phantom II** following the F-100 and prior to the T-38. Pictured in October 2001 at the Castle AFB museum in California is F-4E 66-0289, painted as No 6 of the team.

F-4S Phantom II 157246 is pictured in September 1988 wearing the markings of VMFA-134 at the USMC base at El Toro, California.

The **F-4S Phantom II** was a reworking of the USN/USMC F-4J to include such features as the slatted wing. F-4S 153868 is pictured in October 2001 at the Santa Maria Museum of Flight, California. It is in the toned-down grey markings so prevalent on military aircraft today.

Above left: Such was the success of the F-4 Phantom II in Navy service that the USAF evaluated and then adopted the type. Originally designated F-110, it entered USAF service as the **F-4C**. 64-0776 is displayed at the Museum of Flight at Boeing Field, Washington in May 2000.

Above right: The first Phantom II designed to USAF specifications was the **F-4D**. It had a vast number of internal fittings and equipment changes. 66-7723 is pictured, in May 2000, preserved at Elmendorf AFB, Anchorage, Alaska.

Right: Following lessons learned in the air war over Vietnam the next Phantom, the F-4E, had an internal gun. This was one of many upgrades in what was to become the variant with the largest production run. **NF-4E Phantom II** 66-0329 is at the Pima County Museum, Arizona in October 1998. The 'N' prefix indicates it is a test aircraft modified to such an extent that it would be uneconomical to revert it to stock. Its colour scheme and 'ED' code are from the USAF Test Centre at Edwards AFB.

The first export sale of the Phantom was to the United Kingdom for service with the Fleet Air Arm. The biggest difference from US Navy aircraft was the change of powerplants to a pair of Rolls-Royce Spey turbofan engines. As well as the Royal Navy, the RAF operated the type for many years. **Phantom FGR.2** (F-4M) XV474 is pictured in May 1996, as part of the Imperial War Museum collection at Duxford.

The **Douglas F-5D Skylancer** was a single-seat navy fighter. Despite having a satisfactory performance it was not ordered into production. The four flying aircraft were then used by NACA/NASA as research testbeds. F-5D-1 NASA 802 is displayed at the Neil Armstrong Air & Space Museum at Wapakoneta, Ohio in July 1986. The astronaut and first man on the moon flew this aircraft while a NASA test pilot, the location in Ohio being his home town.

Left: The **Douglas F-6A Skyray** was the first USN fighter capable of a performance of Mach 1 in level flight. A single-seat carrier-borne interceptor powered by a single Pratt & Whitney J57 turbojet of 10,500 lb thrust with afterburner, it had a delta-wing configuration. 134836 is at the New England Museum in Connecticut in July 1986.

Right: A most unconventional aircraft for its day, the **Vought F7U Cutlass** has no tail. It had evolved from captured German research during World War Two. A single-seat carrier-borne fighter, it first flew in 1950 and had a difficult early development. F7U-3 129642 is photographed at Willow Grove NAS, Pennsylvania, in May 1989.

Below: The final sub-version of the **Cutlass** was equipped to carry four Sparrow radar-guided missiles. One such aircraft, F7U-3M 129655, is seen on show in April 1994 at the US Navy Museum at Pensacola.

In the early years of carrier-borne jet operations, the aircraft involved usually had a lower performance than their land-based equivalents. Therefore, it surprised many when a naval fighter took the world air speed record. In October 1953 it was raised to 752mph (1,211km/h) by an XF4D-1 Skyray. 134748, an **F4D-1** (F-6A after 1962), is pictured preserved at Pima County Museum in October 1998.

First flown in 1954, the **Grumman F11F Tiger** entered squadron service in 1957 with VA-156. After only two years it was transferred to the role of advanced trainer. F11F-1 141783 is seen at the prow of the USS *Intrepid* Museum, New York in May 1989.

The most famous user of the **Grumman Tiger** was the US Navy Flight Demonstration Squadron, *The Blue Angels*, who equipped with the type from 1957 until the end of 1968 when the aircraft were replaced by F-4 Phantoms. F11F-1 141884 is seen at Pensacola NAS, Florida in October 1981.

Launched in 1966, the 'Attack Experimental' programme called for a rugged ground-attack aircraft. Two companies eventually were funded to build prototypes for a fly-off against each other. The loser was the **Northrop A-9**. First flown in 1972, both aircraft built have been preserved. YA-9A 71-1367 is pictured in October 1984 at the Castle AFB Museum, California.

The winner of the 'AX' competition was the **Republic A-10**. This design is still in service today, and proved its worth as a ground-attack platform during the 1991 Gulf War. A-10A 75-0298 is seen at the Pima County Museum in October 1998.

Above left: First flown in 1950, the **Douglas F3D Skyknight** was an all-weather, carrier-based fighter with side-by-side seating for the pilot and radar operator. F3D-2 127074 is on deck at the USS *Intrepid* Museum, New York in May 1989.

Above right: The **Skyknight** became the first tactical jet to be converted to the role of electronic warfare while serving with the US Marine Corps. 124618, an F3D-2Q (EF-10B after 1962), is seen at the US Marine Corps Air-Ground Museum at Quantico, Virginia in May 1989.

Left: Vought's **F-8 Crusader** was known as the 'last of the gun fighters' and performed with great success against the MiGs of North Vietnam. First flying in 1955, it was a single-seat supersonic fighter. As well as the USN and USMC, it served with the Philippine Air Force and the French Navy; the latter's aircraft were the last in service, flying until 1999. F-8U-2NE 150920 is in the markings of Marines fighter squadron VMF-323 *Death Rattlers* at El Toro, California in September 1988.

Left: The first Crusader in service was the F8U-1. March 1957 saw the first fleet squadron VF-32 at Cecil Field, Florida. **F-8A** 145336 is at Chino, California in September 1988 as part of the Fighter Jets Collection.

Below: During the lifespan of the Crusader, aircraft were upgraded to new improved specifications as systems evolved. The F-8K was an F-8C thus modified. **F-8K** 145550 is at the Naval Air Warfare Centre, Warminster, Pennsylvania in May 1989.

Thunderbird Aviation of Phoenix, Arizona operated a pair of civil F-8s. They were used for instrument and programme development work as well as the odd airshow. N19TB is seen at Deer Valley, Arizona in October 1998; this aircraft is a hybrid, having the wings of an F-8L fitted to an **F-8K** fuselage. It has been acquired for preservation by Paul Allen and is currently at Arlington, WA.

The distinctive livery of 144427 marks it out as a **DF-8F Crusader**. This variant was a drone controller and flew for the Pacific missile test range at Point Mugu, California. The illustrated example is at the Pima County Museum in October 1998.

Above: First of a long line of carrier-borne jet fighters from Grumman was the **F9F Panther**. It was a straight-wing single-seater powered by a Pratt & Whitney J48 turbojet of 6,250 lbst. The type was the first US Navy jet in combat when it flew in the Korean War. F9F-2 127120 is at Willow Grove NAS, Pennsylvania in May 1989.

Right: Being a relatively simple aircraft the **F9F Panther** can be found in small numbers as a privately-owned warbird. F9F-2B N9525A/123078 is seen at an airshow at Madera, California in August 1986.

Right: The F9F designation was kept for the follow-on fighter from Grumman. This was the swept-wing **Cougar**. Power was still supplied by the J48 but the thrust had increased to 7,250 lb. F9F-7 130763 is at the Cradle of Aviation Museum, Mitchel Field, Long Island, New York in May 1989.

Below: The final version of the Cougar was the F9F-8. This had a small increase in length and modifications to the wing. 712 aircraft of this variant were produced. **F9F-8 Cougar** 131232 is at the Museum of Flight, Boeing Field, Washington in May 2000.

Seen at the Pima County Museum in October 1998 is the photo-reconnaissance version of the Cougar. This has a much increased nose size to house the cameras. The 'P' in the designation of **F9F-8P** 144426 indicates its role.

A two-seat tandem jet trainer variant of the Cougar was produced. This was 34in longer to accommodate the instructor. First flown in 1956, it served until 1974. 141121, an **F9F-8T** (TF-9J after 1962) is seen at the Pima County Museum in October 1998.

One of the most stylish of carrier-borne aircraft was the **North American A-5 Vigilante**. Its Mach 2 performance came from a pair of GE J79 turbojets of 10,800 lbst. With a length of 76ft 6in it was one of the largest fleet-based aircraft. RA-5C 149289 is pictured, in October 1998, as part of the collection at Pima County Museum.

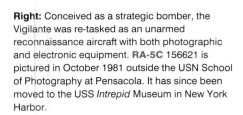

Right: Conceived as a strategic bomber, the Vigilante was re-tasked as an unarmed reconnaissance aircraft with both photographic and electronic equipment. **RA-5C** 156621 is pictured in October 1981 outside the USN School of Photography at Pensacola. It has since been moved to the USS *Intrepid* Museum in New York Harbor.

Above: 1966 saw the US Air Force place orders for the Corsair II. This was the second naval design it purchased in a few short years, the first being the F-4 Phantom. The major difference from the US Navy aircraft was replacement of the powerplant with an Allison TF41, a licence-built Rolls-Royce Spey. **GA-7D** 69-6193 is pictured at Chanute AFB, Illinois in July 1986.

Below: First flying in 1968, the **A-7E Corsair II** was the Navy variant with the new engine used by the USAF. This version was the largest production batch of the type. 156815 is pictured in October 1979 at the gate of NAS Lemoore, California.

In 1963 the US Navy initiated a design competition for an A-4 Skyhawk replacement in the light-attack role. The winner was the **Vought A-7A Corsair II**. The company had used the F-8 Crusader as the starting block to re-engineer the type for the new task. First flown in 1965, it was powered by a single P&W TF30 turbofan. 152658 is seen preserved at the Naval Air Test & Evaluation Museum, Patuxent River, Maryland in May 1989.

Above: Following service with the USAF, including operations at the tail-end of the Vietnam War, the A-7 served in a number of ANG units across America. **A-7D** 69-6202 is preserved by the 198th FS, Puerto Rico ANG at San Juan in November 1992.

Right: The failure of its designed powerplant blighted the service career in the US Navy of the **McDonnell F3H Demon**. The type was a single-seat fighter and the first naval aircraft from this manufacturer to have swept wings. 133566, an F3H-2N (F-3C after 1962), is on deck at the USS *Intrepid* Museum, New York in May 1989.

Below: The **Grumman A-6 Intruder** is a subsonic two-seat, side-by-side, carrier-borne attack bomber used by both the USN and USMC. It has all-weather capability and variants include tanker and electronic warfare airframes. A-6E 155713 is at the Pima County Museum in October 1998.

Bell's **P-59 Airacomet** was America's first jet. Power was provided by the General Electric Type 1, developed from the British Whittle unit. Although armed with both cannon and machine-guns it served as a fighter-trainer. P-59B 44-22633 is displayed at Edwards AFB, California in October 1979, where the type first flew when the base was still known as Muroc AAF.

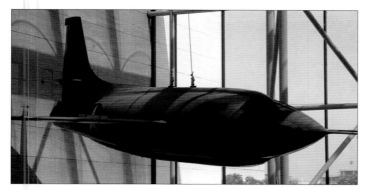

Above left: One of the most significant aircraft of all time is pictured in May 1989 at the National Air & Space Museum in Washington DC. This is the **Bell X-1**, 46-062, in which Captain Charles (Chuck) Yeager was the first person to fly at Mach 1, in October 1947.

Above right: The first aircraft to pass Mach 2 was a **Douglas D-558-2 Skyrocket**. Like the X-1, this was air-launched, in this case from a P2B-1S (US Navy B-29) as the project was Navy-sponsored. 37973, the first Skyrocket to fly, is pictured in September 1988 at the Fighter Jets Collection, Chino, California.

Left: A lightweight, carrier-based, single-seat attack bomber the **Douglas A-4 Skyhawk** had a production run of more than 3,000 airframes. It served the US Navy in many roles and to this day soldiers on in a number of air forces worldwide. A-4C 147727 is pictured at Porterville Airport, California in October 1979.

Right: Still operated by the Republic of Singapore Air Force the **Douglas A-4S Skyhawk** has been updated over the years. 607 is pictured in February 2003 at their museum at Paya Lebar.

Below left: This **A-4C Skyhawk**, N401FS/148571, is pictured, in October 1998, at the gate of the Pima County Museum in Arizona. It is in the house colours of Flight Systems, a Mojave-based company who are now part of BAE Systems.

Below right: This **Skyhawk** is part of a special section in Argentina's national museum at Moron commemorating the role the air force played in the 1982 Malvinas (Falkland Islands) conflict with the UK. C-207, an A-4B, is a survivor from operations against the British fleet. It is pictured in October 2003.

The largest and heaviest aircraft in squadron service that was used for regular operations from the decks of aircraft carriers was the **Douglas A3D Skywarrior**. It was a twin-engined, three-crew bomber that first flew in 1952 at Edwards AFB. YA3D-1 130361 is at the Pima County Museum in October 1998.

The **Douglas B-66 Destroyer** was a direct development of the Skywarrior for the USAF. While looking very similar there were many changes in the new design, including the powerplant. The A3's P&W J57s were replaced by a pair of Allison J71s. RB-66B 53-0412 is part of the collection at Chanute AFB, Illinois in August 1986.

Left: The B-66 found its true role when operated as an electronic reconnaissance/warfare aircraft. This variant had an ECM compartment fitted in place of the bomb bay, which housed four extra crew to operate the equipment. **RB-66B** 53-0475 is at the USAF Museum in Dayton, Ohio in July 1986.

Below: Developed for USAF reconnaissance use rather than the A-12's CIA role, the **Lockheed SR-71** broke many world speed records that will stand for years to come. It flew from New York to London in 1 hour 54 minutes and London to Los Angeles in 3 hours 47 minutes. 64-17958 is at the Warner Robins Museum, Georgia in April 1994.

Below: To replace the U-2 reconnaissance aircraft, the manufacturer Lockheed produced a machine of still-unsurpassed performance. This was the A-12, which first flew from the secret Groom Lake site in Nevada in 1962. To extend its capability over hostile airspace a Lockheed D-21 reconnaissance drone was test-launched from the top of the fuselage. This was not a great success. Pictured at the Museum of Flight, Boeing Field, Washington in May 2000 is **Lockheed A-12MD** 60-6940 with a D-21 fitted.

Still the front-line interceptor for the USAF, the **McDonnell Douglas F-15 Eagle** is a single-seat craft powered by a pair of P&W F100 turbofans giving a thrust of 23,830 lb each with afterburners. First flown in 1972, it entered service two years later with the first two-seaters for instructor training at Luke AFB, Arizona. The early models have begun to find new roles. Illustrated is an example from 3rd Wing at Elmendorf AFB, Alaska, in May 2000.

The US Navy equivalent of the F-15 is the **Grumman F-14 Tomcat**, the last of a long line of Grumman 'Cats' for the Navy. It is a two-seater fleet-defence fighter powered by a pair of P&W TP30 turbofans giving 20,900 lb of thrust with afterburners – the later 'D' model has GE F110 engines. YF-14A 157984 is one of twelve prototypes used for development work. Now preserved, it is at the entrance to the US Navy Museum at Pensacola in April 1994.

The **Northrop F-5** was produced as a lightweight fighter for America's allies who could not afford or did not need the latest and most expensive equipment. It proved to be a great success with production continuing for many years, and it was developed far beyond the capability of the original design. More than twenty nations have operated the type, or still do. YF-5A 59-4987 is seen in the Museum of Flight at Boeing Field, Washington in May 2000.

With many first-generation Harriers out of service and in store, the Pima County Museum in Arizona has obtained its first example. **AV-8A** 159241 is pictured in October 1998 in the markings of USMC squadron VMA-513 *Flying Nightmares*.

Developed from the successful F-5, the **Northrop F-20** was the fighter nobody wanted to buy despite its being a brilliant development. F-20A N44671 is displayed at the Western Museum of Flight at Hawthorne Airport, California. This airfield is also the home base of the Northrop company.

Left: The **Hawker Kestrel** was the first development from the P.1127 research aircraft. This VTOL (Vertical take-off and landing) design was flown by the Kestrel Evaluation Squadron at RAF West Raynham. Its pilots came from the RAF, USAF, US Navy, US Army and Luftwaffe. Following this the airframes were split between the UK and America. XS692/64-18266, a Kestrel F(GA).1 designated XV-6A in the USA, was first used by the US Navy and then by NASA. It is seen as NASA 520 at the Air Power Park, Hampton, Virginia in May 1989.

Below: Convair's **Sea Dart** was a US Navy idea for a fighter based on water to operate with support from ships. It had a large retractable hydro-ski for landing. First flown in 1953 it exceeded the speed of sound the following year. The design never entered production. XF2Y-1 135763 is at the San Diego Aerospace Museum in September 1988.

It is odd to find one of the most modern and advanced military aircraft in a museum. That fate befell the **Northrop YF-23** when it lost the competition to replace the F-15 Eagle to the YF-22. YF-23A 87-0801 is pictured, in October 2001, when on display at the Western Museum of Flight, Hawthorne Airport, Los Angeles.

America's first four-engined jet bomber was the **North American B-45 Tornado**. First flown in 1947, it was a straight-wing tactical bomber with a crew of four. The powerplants were four 5,200 lbst GE J47 turbojets paired in a nacelle under each wing. 47-0008 is pictured, in October 1984, as part of the collection at Castle AFB Museum, California.

Above: Designed in the late 1950s and first flown in 1964, the **North American XB-70 Valkyrie** is perhaps one of the most futuristic-looking aircraft ever. It was a six-engined bomber with a Mach 3+ performance. Only two were produced, as the prevailing view was that it would not survive over Russia with the development of Soviet surface-to-air missiles. 62-001 is at the USAF Museum, Dayton, Ohio in July 1986.

Left: One of the most controversial warplanes of all time was the **General Dynamics F-111**. Most of it was due to politics rather than the aircraft, although its combat career got off to a poor start in 1968 when six aircraft were sent to Vietnam. Three were lost within four weeks, none from enemy action. It did, however, mature into an excellent bombing platform with superb low-flying capability. 63-9766 is the first of the pre-production development aircraft and is seen at the Milestones of Flight Museum, Lancaster, California in October 1979. This airframe has since been moved to the Edwards AFB Museum.

Right: Boeing's **B-52 Stratofortress** was the 'big stick' of the USAF's Strategic Air Command during the Cold War. First flown in 1952 and entering service three years later, it still serves today and is scheduled to do so until 2020, an amazing 65-year life span. RB-52B 52-8711 is pictured in July 1986 at the SAC Museum at Omaha, Nebraska. The RB-52 carried a reconnaissance pod in the bomb bay.

Below: The only other operator of the **Lockheed U-2** was the Chinese Nationalist Air Force. It was used for very high-altitude flights over the Chinese mainland. U-2B 3512/56-6691 is pictured at the Military Museum, Beijing, in December 1987. It had been shot down and the parts re-assembled for public view.

The history of the **Lockheed U-2** dates back to 1954 when the contract was placed for its production. It flew the following year from the Groom Lake site amid great secrecy. Its role was to overfly Russia and, using the most advanced cameras available, photograph strategic sites. Early operations were by the CIA and later the USAF. U-2C 56-6714 is at Beale AFB, California, in October 1984, the home base of the type.

Left: With power from eight engines and its high-wing design, the B-52 was a natural choice for the role of 'mother plane' for a number of the 'X' series of NASA rocket aircraft. **NB-52A** 52-0003 was used for the X-15 project and is pictured at the Pima County Museum in October 1998.

Below: It is not very common to find the prototypes of many 1950s aircraft preserved. The second prototype **Boeing XB-47** is one of the exceptions. It first flew in 1947 fitted with J47 engines; the first aircraft having been powered by Allison J35s. 46-0066/'2278' is pictured at Chanute AFB, Illinois in August 1986.

Boeing's other multi-engined bomber for SAC was the **B-47 Stratojet**. It was six-engined, with GE J47s of 6,000 lbst each. The service life was much shorter than the B-52; starting in 1951 it was over by the end of the 1960s. B-47E 53-2385 is pictured guarding the gate at Plattsburg AFB in upstate New York in July 1986.

The last **Boeing B-47E** to fly was 52-0166, which was delivered to the Castle AFB Museum in California. It is seen carrying the name *Spirit* at that location in September 1988.

Above: SAC's first supersonic bomber was the **Convair B-58 Hustler**. It had a maximum speed of 1,385mph with a service ceiling of 63,000ft and a crew of three. It had a short service life lasting from 1960 to 1970. 61-2080 is pictured in October 1998 at the Pima County Museum, Arizona.

Right: As well as a bomber variant of the Hustler, Convair developed a reconnaissance version, the RB-58, with special equipment being housed in the underslung pod. The type was cancelled and only the bomber went into service. **YRB-58A Hustler** 55-0666/'12059' is one of thirteen test aircraft; this one is pictured at Chanute AFB, Illinois in August 1986.

Being so far ahead of any other aircraft in its class, the English Electric Canberra was adopted for operational service with the USAF. American aircraft were built under licence as the **Martin B-57**. Since the Canberra has such a superb altitude performance a reconnaissance variant was one of the earliest service types. RB-57A 52-1475 is at Warner Robins AFB, Georgia in April 1994.

Defence Systems Evaluation Squadrons of the USAF operated an electronic warfare variant of the B-57. This provided training for both air and ground-based personnel. **EB-57B** 52-1526 is at Beale AFB Museum, California in October 1984.

Left: Some aircraft preservation does not involve a museum or a flying life. This **Martin WB-57A**, N1005/52-1419, is pictured in October 1981, when it was in use by the George T Baker School at Miami for training aircraft engineers.

Below: The most radical versions of the B-57 were the big-wing, ultra-high-altitude, strategic reconnaissance platforms. The wingspan was increased from 64ft to 122ft 5in and an extra engine, a P&W J60 turbojet of 2,900 lbst, was added to the underside of each wing. The aircraft were later designated **WB-57F** after their role became one of weather reconnaissance. NASA used several aircraft for research at the Johnson Space Flight Centre at Houston. N925NA is pictured at the Pima County Museum in October 1998.

The **N20 Aiguillon** is one of several types of Swiss-designed and -built combat aircraft, none of which reached production status. The sole example is pictured at the air force museum at Dubendorf in September 2004.

Powered by a licence-built Rolls-Royce Avon engine, the **Saab J32 Lansen** first flew in November 1952. Its role was as an all-weather day- and night-fighter. Service entry was in 1956. Final duties were as target-tugs and electronic warfare trainers. J32E 32543 is pictured at the Museo del Aire, Madrid in September 2002.

Neutral Sweden has long provided its air force with the most advanced warplanes from its own national aircraft industry. The **Saab J35 Draken** produced a Mach 2 performance from a single Swedish-built Rolls-Royce Avon turbojet. This interceptor has just finished its last days of front-line service with the Austrian Air Force. Seen at the Royal Army Museum, Brussels, in June 1983, is J35B 35067 in its original markings.

Left: Nicknamed *The Flying Barrel*, the **Saab J29** was Sweden's first swept-wing jet. It served in a variety of roles and was exported to Austria. It was first flown in September 1948; entered service with the Swedish Air Force in May 1951; and ended its career as a target-tug in August 1976. Pictured in April 2005, as a gate guard for F21 Wing at Lulea in Sweden's far north, is J29C 29929.

Below left: Spanish jet trainer **Hispano HA-200 Saeta** was first flown in 1955, the design and production having been supervised by Professor Messerschmitt. Powered by a pair of 880 lbst Turboméca Marboré turbojets, it has proved to be a popular private warbird in the USA. N5486J is seen at an airshow at Lakeland, Florida in April 1994.

Below right: 2005 saw the withdrawal from service with the Swedish Air Force of the **Saab J37 Viggen** (Thunderbolt). This was a defence-cut decision as the aircraft still had a lot of life in it. The last wing flying them was F21 at Lulea. Prior to this selected museums had received examples. Pictured, in September 2002, at the Museo del Aire, Madrid is AJS37 37074. This variant was multi-role in attack, fighter and reconnaissance operations.

Above left: Designed as a light-strike and reconnaissance fighter for NATO, the Fiat G91 was only purchased new by the manufacturing nation and Germany. The most high-profile user of the G91 was the Italian Air Force *Frecce Tricolori* aerobatic team. **Fiat G91PAN** MM6244 is pictured at the Museum of Flight at Boeing Field, Washington in May 2000.

Above right: Avro Canada designed and produced the **CF-100** as a two-seat all-weather fighter. As well as seeing Canadian service, it was bought by the Belgian Air Force. 18506 is displayed at Hamilton, Ontario in June 1990.

Right: The aviation industry of the People's Republic of China has often produced licensed copies of Russian aircraft. One such is the **Xian F-7**, a version of the early MiG-21F. '0003 red' is seen at the Beijing Aviation Institute in December 1987.

The **Harbin H-5** is a Chinese-produced Ilyushin IL-28. This twin-engined, straight-wing tactical bomber was first flown by the Russians in 1948. '10198 red' is in the China Aviation Museum at Datang Shan, near Beijing in October 1999.

Soviet two-seat conversion training aircraft are some of the ugliest to be seen. The two-pilot IL-28U was first flown in 1950 and features an extra cockpit. '10692 red' is a **Harbin HJ-5**, a Chinese-built version. It is at the China Aviation Museum near Beijing in October 1999.

Above left: China's first indigenous fighter was the **Shenyang J-8**. First flown in 1970, it had a long development with the first production version, the J-8I, not flying for another eleven years. It is thought that the total build was about fifty airframes, most of which have been used to test equipment. J-8I '72061 red' is seen at the China Aviation Museum in October 1999.

Above right: For many years the backbone of the Chinese Air Force was the **Shenyang J-6**. This was its version of the MiG-19 in its fighter role. This example is at the China Aviation Museum in October 1999.

Right: The most successful of China's recent production is the re-working of the MiG-19 into the **Nanchang Q-5** (Attack Aircraft No 5). The fuselage was stretched and the air intakes repositioned to the sides of the cockpit. It has been exported to eleven nations including Pakistan. Q-5IA '10769 red' is pictured, in October 1999, in the China Aviation Museum.

An earlier service aircraft was the **Shenyang J-5**, this being the Chinese version of the MiG-17 fighter. '2579 red' is pictured, in October 1999, at the China Aviation Museum. It has a 'kill' marking, as this particular aircraft shot down a Grumman HU-16 Albatross.

Two examples of the **Nanchang J-12** lightweight fighter project are to be found in the China Aviation Museum. One is on a pole outside, the other inside: it is pictured in October 1999.

Three versions of the **Sud-Ouest SO 4050 Vautour** were produced; a tactical-attack aircraft, a light bomber and an all-weather fighter. First flown in 1952, it served with the French Air Force until the 1980s, its last role being that of a target-tug. Power for all versions was provided by a pair of SNECMA Atar turbojets of 7,720 lbst each. No 347, a Vautour IIN fighter version, is pictured, in May 1977, at the gate of the air force base at Reims/Champagne.

Powered by a licence-built Rolls-Royce Nene turbojet of 5,070 lbst, the **Dassault MD450 Ouragan** was a straight-wing subsonic fighter for the French Air Force. First flown in 1949, it also served with the air forces of India and Israel. No 150 is at the Musée de l'Air in Paris in May 1983.

Left: First flown in 1952, the **Dassault Mystère IVA** was the follow-on fighter after the Ouragan. This design had a swept wing and a subsonic performance. It too was sold to India and Israel. It is one of the latter air force's aircraft that is on show at the national museum of Chile in Santiago. No 29 is pictured without any air force markings in October 2003.

Below: With its distinctive butterfly tail the **Aérospatiale (Fouga) CM170 Magister** has been one of France's most successful exports in the jet trainer field. More than fifteen nations have used the type or still do so. This aircraft was not equipped with an ejector seat. FM21 is one of a pair, pictured in June 1998, mounted on poles at the Finnish Air Force training base at Kauhava.

Above: France developed a number of research aircraft during the 1950s, including the **Nord N1500 Griffon**. This was one of a series of experiments in mixed power, its normal turbojet being augmented by a ram-jet to boost performance in the interceptor role. None of these aircraft entered service. No 2 is at the Musée de l'Air in May 1983.

Right: In the fighter role France's most successful aircraft was the **Dassault Mirage III**. A Mach 2 interceptor, it achieved fame and a boost to its sales with the performance of Israeli Air Force machines during the 1967 'Six-Day War'. C.11-09, a Mirage IIIEE version optimised for strike and attack, is pictured in Spanish Air Force colours at the Museo del Aire, Cuatro Vientos, Madrid in September 2002.

Left: The **Boulton Paul P.IIIA** was a delta-wing research aircraft. First flown in 1950, it was powered by a single Rolls-Royce Nene turbojet of 5,100 lbst. Most of its flying career was at the Royal Aircraft Establishment, Bedford, as part of the Aerodynamics Flight. It was grounded in 1958. VT935 is seen at the Midland Air Museum, Coventry in November 2001.

Below: One of the most historic British aircraft is pictured, in February 1990, at the Science Museum in London. This is the **Gloster E28/39** W4041/G, the first British jet-propelled aircraft. Power was supplied by a single Whittle W1 turbojet giving 1,700 lbst. The momentous first flight was at RAF Cranwell on 15th May 1941 in the hands of test pilot Gerry Sayer.

Designed as a high-speed research aircraft, the **Bristol 188** was made out of stainless steel and powered by a pair of de Havilland Gyron Junior turbojets of 10,000 lbst each. The aircraft was intended to cruise at Mach 2.5 but problems with the engines and a limited fuel capacity saw the type reach only Mach 1.88. XF926/8368M is pictured at the RAF Museum, Cosford in June 2002.

The **Supermarine 510** was a development aircraft that bridged the gap between the straight-wing Attacker and the later Swift. It retained the tailwheel undercarriage of the former. VV106 is pictured, in July 1975, at RAF Colerne. It is now part of the FAA Museum at Yeovilton.

Above: Not many jet aircraft have fixed undercarriages but since the **Handley Page HP.115** was designed for low-speed research into delta wings for the Concorde project it was decided not to complicate it. Like the P.111A above, it spent most of its life at the RAE, Bedford. XP841 is now part of the 'Concorde Collection' at the Fleet Air Arm Museum at Yeovilton, and is pictured there in July 1985.

Right: Another pure research aircraft, the **Hunting H.126** was used to explore low-speed jet-flaps. The single Bristol Siddeley Orpheus turbojet passed its exhaust through the full wing-span flaps and tail nozzles. First flown in 1963, it served until the end of the decade. XN714 is seen with the RAF Museum, Cosford in August 1994.

Above left: Mixed-power projects of jets and rocket engines were explored in the 1950s and the **Saunders-Roe SR.53** was one such design. First flown in 1957, it was to have led to the production fighter SR.177. This was cancelled along with many others in the infamous 1957 Defence White Paper from Duncan Sandys, who predicted that all fighter needs could be met by missiles! XD145 is pictured at the RAF Museum, Cosford in May 1989.

Above right: The **Fairey Delta II** gained worldwide fame when, on 10th March 1956 with Peter Twiss at the controls, it became the first aircraft to exceed 1,000mph when it took the World Absolute Speed Record up to 1,132mph. The margin over the previous record has not been bettered since. WG777/7986M is seen, in April 1991, at the RAF Museum, Cosford.

Left: The actual world speed record-holder FD2 was converted into the **BAC 221**. This aircraft was to test the ogee-wing planform of the Concorde in high-speed flight. It first flew in this guise in 1964. WG774 is pictured, in August 1984, at the FAA Museum, Yeovilton, where it forms part of the 'Concorde Collection'.

With the Vulcan project in mind, Avro constructed a small number of delta-wing research aircraft as the **Avro 707**. The first one flew in 1949 and the last was retired in 1967. They had been used for a number of different research projects. 707A WD280 was shipped to Australia and used for tests of airflow over delta wings. It is pictured at the RAAF Museum at Point Cook in February 2003.

Above: The quest for a practical VTOL aircraft has troubled designers for years. The early ones had a set of 'lift engines' and another set for 'forward flight'. This weight cost of a complete set of powerplants used only for take-off and landing was not resolved until the rotary nozzles of the P.1127. The **Short SC.1** was built in the mid-1950s with two sets of engines. It first flew in 1957 as a conventional aircraft, and in the following year in a VTOL mode. XG900 is pictured at Yeovilton in July 1994; although it is now part of the collection at the Science Museum, London.

Right: Hawker's **P.1127** proved to be the first practical VTOL aircraft. This was thanks to the use of a single engine with moveable nozzles to transit from vertical to forward flight. The powerplant was a Bristol Siddeley Pegasus. First flown in 1960, it evolved into the Kestrel and then the service Harrier. XP980 is pictured at the FAA Museum, Yeovilton in July 1994.

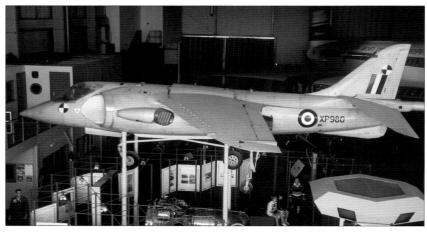

In the latter years of World War Two Saunders-Roe looked at the concept of a jet-fighter flying-boat to be used in the advance across the Pacific Ocean against the Japanese forces. The resulting design, the **Saro SRA.1**, did not in fact fly until 1947, by which time the aircraft had no role. TG263 is pictured at Staverton in May 1975. It is now part of the Imperial War Museum collection at Duxford.

Above: The first jet in squadron service with the Fleet Air Arm was the **Supermarine Attacker**. A single-seat straight-wing carrier-based fighter, it was powered by a single Rolls-Royce Nene with 5,000 lbst. First flown in 1946, it entered service with 800 Squadron in 1951. WA473 is seen at the FAA Museum, Yeovilton in July 1985.

Left: In the years following World War Two, the aviation industry in Argentina was at its most innovative. They produced, in 1947, the Rolls-Royce Derwent-powered **I.Ae.27 Pulqui I**. The name is Indian for 'dart' or 'arrow'. The design by Frenchman Émile Dewoitine was not deemed to be a success and it did not go into production. C-001 is pictured at the national museum at Moron, Buenos Aires in October 2003.

Right: The **Pulqui II** was designed by the German, Prof. Dipl. Ing. Kurt Tank. His most famous aircraft was the Focke-Wulf 190 fighter. This aircraft was developed from his World War Two Ta 183 jet that never got beyond the drawing board. Tank himself flew many of the test flights and, although the design was a success, only six aircraft were built. Pulqui II 1A.X.33 is pictured, in October 2003, as part of Argentina's national collection at Moron.

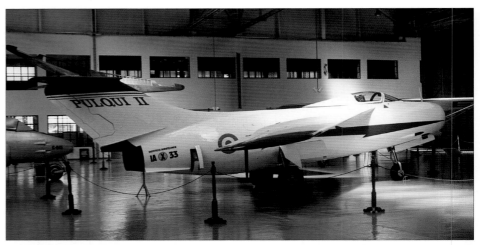

Below: One of the greatest 'what might have been' scenarios was the **BAC TSR.2**: an ultra-low-level strategic bomber first flown in 1964 and cancelled the following year. Power was from a pair of Bristol Siddeley Olympus engines each producing 30,000 lb of thrust with afterburner. XR222, one of the unflown prototypes, is pictured as part of the Imperial War Museum collection at Duxford in May 1996.

A multi-role machine, the **Supermarine Scimitar** was a fighter, a reconnaissance platform and a low-level nuclear-strike aircraft. Power for this carrier-based machine came from a pair of Rolls-Royce Avons. First flown in 1956, it entered operational service two years later. XD317 is seen preserved at the FAA Museum in July 1988.

In 1953 the **Hawker Sea Hawk** replaced the Attacker in FAA service in the ground-attack role. A straight-wing single-seater, it was powered by a Rolls-Royce Nene of 5,200 lbst. WM969/A2530, an FB.5, is part of the IWM collection at Duxford in July 1991.

During 1978 a **Sea Hawk FGA.6** was restored to flying condition as part of the FAA Historic Flight at Yeovilton. WV908 is seen at an airshow at RAF Brawdy in May 1980.

The **Avro Vulcan** was one of the three V-bomber types that saw service in the RAF. First flown in 1952, it entered service as the B.1 in 1957. The B.2 followed in 1960. It saw active service in its last years during the 1982 Falklands War. XM605, a Vulcan B.2, is pictured, in October 1984, at Castle AFB, California.

RAF Bomber Command and the USAF's Strategic Air Command were close partners during the Cold War. It is therefore fitting that **Vulcan B.2** XM573 should be seen, in July 1986, displayed at the SAC Museum at Omaha, Nebraska.

The crescent-winged **Handley Page Victor B.1** was the third of the V-bombers. It first flew in 1952, and joined the RAF in 1957. When the B.2 entered service the B.1s were converted to tankers. Victor K.1A XH592/8429M is at the RAF Museum, Cosford in May 1989.

Above: First of the V-bombers in service was the **Vickers Valiant**. It entered service with the RAF in 1955 and was used in anger during the brief Suez Crisis the following year. Metal fatigue was discovered in the fleet and it was withdrawn at the beginning of 1965. Valiant BK.1 XD816 is seen at RAF Abingdon for the 50th Anniversary Display in June 1968. The nose of this aircraft is now preserved at Brooklands, the original home of Vickers.

Left: 1962 saw the service entry of the **Victor B.2**. The life of the bomber versions was short, being phased out by the end of 1968. The airframes were then converted to tankers and they then had the longest service life of any of the three V-bomber types. Active service was seen during both the Falklands and Gulf Wars. The last squadron on the type, No 55, disbanded in October 1993. Victor K.2 XL231 is part of the Handley Page Collection at the Yorkshire Air Museum, Elvington in July 1997.

The **Folland Gnat T.1** saw RAF service as an advanced trainer with 4 FTS at Valley. Since leaving operations a number have been sold to private pilots. G-MOUR/XR991 is in the colours of *The Yellowjacks*, the first RAF team to use the type. It is seen at an airshow at North Weald in May 1992.

Most famous users of the **Folland Gnat** were the RAF's *Red Arrows*. They flew the trainer from 1965 until its replacement by the Hawk in 1980. G-BVPP/XP504 is a privately-owned example painted in Red Arrows livery as XR993. It is seen at an airshow at Coventry in August 2000.

Left: India and Finland operated the single-seat **Folland Gnat F.1** in squadron strength. The former used the type in its conflicts with Pakistan. GN-103 of the Finnish Air Force is seen, in June 1998, displayed in the town of Kuorevesi.

Right: The **Gloster Javelin** was an RAF two-seat all-weather fighter with delta wings. Javelin FAW.1 XA564/7464M is pictured, in May 1989, at the RAF Museum, Cosford. The type entered service in 1956 and operated until 1968.

Below: Built by de Havilland, the **Sea Vixen** was a two-seat, carrier-borne, all-weather interceptor armed with four Firestreak, later Red Top, homing missiles. No 892 was the first squadron to commission with the FAW.1 in 1959, and the last, No 899, disbanded with the FAW.2 in 1972. Sea Vixen FAW.2 XN692 is a gate guard at RNAS, Yeovilton in July 1988.

Powered by a pair of 880 lbst Turboméca Marboré turbojets the **Morane-Saulnier MS.760 Paris** first flew in July 1954. Its role was as a four-seat high-speed liaison aircraft. Pictured in October 2003, guarding the gate at Argentina's national collection at Moron is MS.760 E-218.

Right: One of the most versatile aircraft of all time is the **English Electric Canberra**. First flown in 1949, it still serves in small numbers with the RAF. It has performed almost every task except that of troop transport! VH-ZQN/A84-234 is an Australian privately-owned B.2. It is pictured about to display at Avalon, Victoria, in February 2003.

Below: Preserved at the Newark Aircraft Museum, in August 1997, is **Canberra B.2/8** WV787/8799M. It is a hybrid model and spent much of its life as a trials aircraft with the RAF. Tasks included spraying water to perform ice trials on other types.

Above: Still in service with the RAF as a reconnaissance platform, the **Canberra PR.9** has a very high-altitude performance with a ceiling of 70,000ft. XH171/8746M is a retired example at the RAF Museum at Cosford in May 1993.

Left: Britain's first swept-wing fighter to enter service was the **Supermarine Swift**. Powered by a single Rolls-Royce Avon turbojet, as a fighter it had a short career, being supplanted by the superior Hawker Hunter. It was however a success in the role of tactical reconnaissance, serving in the 2nd TAF/RAF Germany, until 1961. Swift FR.5 WK281/7712M is pictured at RAF St Athan in September 1983. This aircraft is now part of the Tangmere Military Aviation Museum in West Sussex.

Below left: As an early basic jet trainer the **Jet Provost** found limited success in the export field. Venezuela operated fifteen aircraft until the late 1970s when they were replaced by the T-2 Buckeye. Jet Provost T.52 6780 is mounted outside the Venezuelan Air Force Museum at Maracay in November 1992.

Above: First flown in 1954, the **Hunting Jet Provost** was derived from the earlier Piston Provost. Its role was to provide the RAF with a jet-powered basic trainer so pilots could have a seamless transfer from basic to advanced flying. The prototype T.1 XD674/7570M is seen with the RAF Museum, Cosford in May 1989.

Left: The main production block of the **Jet Provost** was the T.3 to T.5. The biggest difference to the T.1 was a much shorter undercarriage. The final variant was the T.5, which had a pressurised cockpit to cope better with high-altitude training flights. Since being replaced by the Tucano, many JPs have been sold to the private flyer. G-VIVM/XS230, a T.5B, is seen at an airshow at Fairford in July 1996.

Like many basic and advanced training aircraft, the Jet Provost was developed into a light-attack aircraft. This was the **BAC 167 Strikemaster**. The engine remained the Bristol Siddeley Viper but was uprated to provide 3,410 lb of thrust, and eight wing hardpoints were added. More than ten air forces have operated the type or still do. Private owners have purchased some of the surplus military machines. N167SM, a Mk 81, is an ex-South Yemen and Singapore Air Force example and operates in Kenyan markings. It is pictured at Lakeland, Florida in April 1994.

Britain's most successful jet fighter in the 1950s, in terms of both quality and export sales, was the **Hawker Hunter**. First flown in 1951 by Squadron Leader Neville Duke at Boscombe Down, the type can still be found in military service today. WB188/7154M, the P.1067 prototype, has been preserved. Pictured at RAF St Athan in September 1983, it is now part of the Tangmere Military Aviation Museum.

The **Hunter F.4** was the first variant in volume production with 365 being produced. It was also the first to be exported. F.4/Mk 51 N72602 is an ex-Danish Air Force example, now privately owned in America and based at Mojave, California, where it is pictured in October 1984.

Peru was one of many countries that operated **Hunters**. It purchased sixteen ex-RAF F.4s as F.52s in 1956 and flew them until 1980. 137 is at the Peruvian Air Force Museum at Las Palmas, Lima in September 1997.

Above: Improved flying controls and a more powerful Rolls-Royce Avon with 10,000 lbst made the Hunter F.6 a favourite with pilots. It became the standard day fighter for the RAF and was the basis for the airframes converted to become **Hunter FGA.9s**. The air force of Chile was a recipient of some surplus RAF aircraft and have preserved 744 at the Museo Nacional de Aeronautica de Chile at Los Cerrillos, Santiago. It is pictured on outdoor display in October 2003.

Right: One of the most interesting preservation projects is that of the Royal Jordanian Air Force Historic Flight. It operates a number of aircraft types that the air force had flown. One is **Hunter F.58** G-BWKC (an ex-Swiss Air Force machine). It flies with the markings 712/E and is pictured about to display at Fairford in July 1997.

Early **Hunter** pilots converted to type without the aid of a two-seat trainer. The T.7 trainer was first flown in 1955 and served as an advanced trainer for many years as well as carrying out secondary roles including test pilot training for inverted spinning. G-BOOM is a privately-owned example in an all-red scheme. It is pictured at an airshow at Liverpool-Speke in August 1984, and has since joined the RJAF Historic Flight.

1960 saw the RAF enter the Mach 2+ era with the introduction of the **English Electric Lightning F.1** into squadron service with 74 (Tiger) Squadron at Coltishall. Pictured at Duxford, in July 1992, is XM135 in this unit's markings; it is owned by the Imperial War Museum.

Above: A clipped fin top is the mark of the F.3 and F.6 variants of the **Lightning**. These could also fire Red Top missiles in place of Firestreaks. XP748, an F.3, is in the markings of 5 Squadron at the last Lightning base, RAF Binbrook, in September 1977. Following the base's closure it became a target on a firing range in Wales.

Right: Saudi Arabia was one of the export customers for the Lightning. At the end of its service life it was traded in as part of the purchase of Tornado bombers and fighters. Various plans for re-sale were looked at including one for the Austrian Air Force, but they came to nothing. The aircraft were given RAF serials and either sold privately or given to museums. **Lightning F.53** ZF593 is in the markings of 29 Squadron and is at Warner Robins AFB, Georgia in April 1994.

First flown in 1954, the **English Electric P.1A** was the first turbojet to go supersonic in level flight. It led directly to the Lightning fighter. WG763/7816M is seen on gate guard duties at RAF Henlow in May 1979. It has since moved to the Museum of Science and Industry in Manchester.

Above: Flight-refuelling came to the **Lightning** fleet with the F.1A model; XM192 is pictured at the gate of RAF Wattisham in August 1975, in the colours of 111 Squadron. When the base was transferred to the Army, this airframe moved to the Bomber County Aviation Museum at Hemswell in Lincolnshire.

Below: The two-seat **Lightning T.4** trainer was first flown in 1959, with service deliveries beginning two years later. It had side-by-side seating and full mission capability. XL629 guards the gate at RAE Boscombe Down in June 1977.

A high-speed low-level strike aircraft developed for the Royal Navy, the **Blackburn Buccaneer** joined the 'Senior Service' in 1961 with 700Z Flight. Power was provided by a pair of de Havilland Gyron Junior jets of 7,100 lbst. Buccaneer S.1 XK488 is with the FAA Museum, Yeovilton in July 1985.

Above: Following the cancellation of the TSR.2, and then its supposed replacement the F-111K, the RAF adopted the Buccaneer – an aircraft it had been trying to avoid at all costs. It soon realised what an excellent machine it was in the low-level role, and it served from 1969 to 1994. The RAF operated the S.2 variant and this had the more powerful Rolls-Royce Spey with 11,100 lbst each. **Buccaneer S.2B** XX901 is in the 'desert pink' it wore in the 1991 Gulf War, and is seen at the Yorkshire Air Museum, Elvington in July 1997.

Left: Since the **Buccaneer** was a large aircraft it was used as a test-bed for a number of different projects over its lifetime. XW986, an S.2B, is in the RAE's 'Raspberry Ripple' scheme at Kemble, in August 1999, where it was privately-owned.

Right: The Gloster Meteor had two major firsts in its career. It was the RAF's first jet fighter in service and it was the only Allied jet to see active service during World War Two. The prototype **F9/40 Meteor** is DG202/G. The 'G' suffix on the serial indicated a secret aircraft to be guarded at all times while on the ground. It is pictured with the RAF Museum at Cosford in May 1989.

Below: Argentina was among the earliest of the many users of the **Meteor**. The Argentine Air Force operated one hundred. C-041, an F.4, was one of a batch of ex-RAF machines. It is pictured, in October 2003, at the Museo Nacional de Aeronautica at Moron, Buenos Aires.

Until replaced by the Hunter in the mid-1950s the **Meteor F.8** was the standard RAF day fighter. It was powered by a pair of Rolls-Royce Derwent turbojets with 3,600 lbst each. One of the last to serve with the RAF, VZ467 is now privately-owned in Australia as VH-MBX and has the markings of Korean War aircraft A77-851. It is pictured at Avalon in February 2003.

Many **Meteor** airframes were used for test purposes and some of these have been preserved. WK935/7869M was an F.8 converted to have an extra pilot in the nose flying it from a prone position. This was to see if the method could reduce the effects of 'G' (gravity) on the pilot in tight manoeuvres. The project was eventually cancelled after nearly 100 flights. Pictured at RAF Colerne in July 1975, this aircraft is now at the RAF Museum, Cosford.

Despite the aircraft being in service since 1944 there was no **Meteor** trainer until the T.7 flew in 1948. Service entry in the advanced training role was the following year. This variant was not equipped with an ejector seat. WA591 is seen as gate guard at RAF Woodvale in May 1984, where the type was flown until the early 1970s. It was later replaced as gate guard by an F-4 Phantom II.

Another **Meteor** that was adapted for a test role was WA634. This was a T.7 fitted with an F.8 tail. The reason for this was the fitting in the rear seat of a Martin-Baker ejector seat. The airframe was used for a number of years by this company for tests of various marks of seat. Now at the RAF Museum, Cosford, it is seen here at RAF St Athan in September 1983.

The **Meteor FR.9** was a photo-reconnaissance fighter with an extended nose for the cameras. The Ecuadorian Air Force purchased twelve ex-RAF aircraft in 1954 and flew them for many years. FF-123 is at the air force museum at Quito, in September 1997, in the markings of an aerobatic unit that operated them.

Left: A two-seat radar-equipped night-fighter development of the Meteor, the **NF.11** first entered service with the RAF in 1951. Recognisable by its extended nose, G-LOSM/WM167 is a privately-owned and flown example. It is seen at an airshow at Coventry in August 2000.

Below: Too late to see World War Two operations, the **de Havilland Vampire** entered RAF service in 1946. Power for the early models was provided by the de Havilland Goblin with 3,100 lbst. That year the Swedish Air Force was the first foreign air arm to use British jets when the first of 70 was delivered. A number were sold on to the Dominican Air Force in 1952 where they served as fighter-bombers. Vampire F.1 FAD 2714 is pictured, in November 1992, at the air force headquarters in the capital Santo Domingo.

Swiss designed and built, the **FFA** (Flug- und Fahrzeugwerke) **P.16** was a single-seat ground-attack fighter. It first flew in April 1955 but was lost shortly afterwards. A second loss, of the third prototype, caused the program to be cancelled and Hawker Hunters purchased. Pictured at the Swiss Air Force Museum at Dubendorf, in September 2004, is X-HB-VAD.

Venezuela purchased the **Vampire FB.5** in 1952. This variant was optimised for ground-attack work with wing hardpoints for rockets or bombs. 3C-35 is with the air force museum at Maracay in November 1992.

Above: The **Vampire FB.9** was the tropical variant of the FB.5, with an air-conditioning unit to keep the cockpit cool. WL505/7705M is seen at RAF St Athan in September 1983; it is now owned by de Havilland Aviation of Bridgend, South Wales.

Left: The RCAF received the first of its 85 de Havilland Vampires at the start of 1948. By the end of 1956 they had been phased out, the type having been in front-line service for only a short time before being replaced by the Sabre. For much of its life, its role had been as a transitional trainer with the Central Flying School. **Vampire F.3** 17012 is pictured, in August 2005, at the Canadian Museum of Flight & Transportation at Langley, British Columbia.

When the two-seat **Vampire T.11** trainer was introduced into RAF service in 1952, it became the first jet aircraft on which pilots qualified to 'wings' standard. The last RAF operator was the Central Flying School, which kept a Vampire and a Meteor trainer as an airshow attraction under the banner of *The Vintage Pair*. Vampire T.11 XH304 is pictured displaying at Liverpool-Speke in August 1984.

Above: Another aircraft in the fleet of the Royal Jordanian Air Force Historic Flight is **Vampire T.55** G-BVLM/209. This is an ex-Swiss Air Force machine and is pictured displaying at RAF Fairford in July 1995.

Right: Switzerland is the source of a number of flying warbirds on the airshow circuit. The **de Havilland Venom** was a follow-on development from the Vampire in the role of a fighter-bomber, which was powered by a single DH Goblin engine. G-DHUU/WR410 is an ex-Swiss Venom FB.50 and is seen at an airshow at RAF Fairford in July 1998.

The **Venom FB.4** was a development of the FB.1 and additions included hydraulically-operated ailerons. 8C-36 is a Venezuelan example in the air force museum at Maracay in November 1992.

Russia's first two jet fighters made maiden flights on the same day at the same airfield, Zhukovsky. It was 24th April 1946 and the two aircraft were the **MiG-9** and the Yak-15. The first on the day was the MiG, later allotted the NATO codename *Fargo*. '01 red' is at the Air Force Academy Museum, Monino, near Moscow in August 1995.

One of the first MiGs to be put through its paces in the West was the very nimble **MiG-29** fighter (NATO codename *Fulcrum*). It has a top speed of Mach 2+ and is in service with more than 25 air forces. '04 blue' is at the Central Air & Space Museum at Khodinka Airport, Moscow in August 1995.

Russia's MiG-23 is a swing-wing, single-seat interceptor. A Mach 2 performance is delivered by a single Tumanskii R29 turbojet of 25,348 lb thrust with afterburner. Pictured at the Luftfahrthistorische Sammlung Flugplatz, Finow, Germany is ex-DDR-operated **MiG-23UB** 20+57, a two-seat conversion trainer; it is known by NATO as the *Flogger*.

The **MiG-29** can also be configured for ground-attack roles. '26 blue' is on display at the Museum of the Great Patriotic War in Moscow in August 1995.

Basing it on the MiG-23, the Mikoyan OKB (Design Bureau) produced the **MiG-27** as a dedicated ground-attack aircraft. The biggest external differences are the re-shaped nose and the small air intake plates. '01 yellow' is at the Monino Museum in August 1995. NATO uses the reporting name *Flogger* for this type as well.

A Mach 3+ fighter, the **MiG-25** (*Foxbat*) was designed with the task of intercepting the North American B-70. This bomber was cancelled but the MiG went ahead and served as a fighter in limited numbers. With its size and speed it was not very manoeuvrable. It did however use these characteristics to its advantage in the role of a photographic-reconnaissance platform as its service ceiling of nearly 70,000ft plus its speed made it a difficult machine to intercept. MiG-25R '55 red' is at the Central Air & Space Museum, Moscow in August 1995. Note the camera ports in the nose.

Above left: With the high performance of the MiG-25, a dedicated two-seat trainer was required. This first appeared in 1968 and had an extra cockpit in the nose for the instructor. **MiG-25U** '90 blue' is at the Central Air & Space Museum, Moscow in August 1995.

Above right: The family line from the MiG-25 can be detected in the **MiG-31** (*Foxhound*). It is a long-range, single-seat, high-speed interceptor fighter. '96 black' is at the Monino Museum in August 1995.

Left: **Mikoyan's Ye-166** was an experimental aircraft that captured both a world height and speed record in 1962. The sole aircraft, E166, is pictured at the Monino Museum in August 1991.

Above left: Starting as a simple lightweight fighter, the MiG-21 has grown into a multi-role machine that even today is being upgraded with the latest avionics. The first export customer was Finland, with fighter squadron HävLLv 31 at Rissala receiving aircraft from April 1963. **MiG-21F** MG-61 is pictured at Kuopto Airport in June 1998.

Above right: Seen at the Museum of Flight, Boeing Field in May 2000 is **MiG-21PFM** 5411 in the markings of the Czech Air Force. Known to NATO as the *Fishbed-F*, this variant had a redesigned canopy, powerplant and radar.

Right: With the vast number of MiG-21 airframes built, it is only natural that some would be modified for various test roles. One is the **MiG-21 Analog**. This had its wing shape changed to an ogival-delta for work on the Tupolev Tu-144 supersonic airliner. It is pictured at the Monino Museum in August 1995.

Left: The third generation of the *Fishbed* is the **MiG-21***bis*. The built-up spine is the most noticeable external difference; there are many internal changes. '838 red' heads a line of preserved MiGs at the Luftfahrttechnischer Museumverein Rothenburg, Germany in May 2004. The enthusiasts who run this museum are former DDR MiG instructor pilots.

Below: It was felt in Russia that the jump from the two-seat MiG-15UTI to the single-seat MiG-21 was too great, there being no two-seat MiG-17s or -19s. The first MiG-21U trainer (NATO codename *Mongol*) flew in 1960. Most of the nearly 50 air forces that flew MiG-21s operated two-seaters. Ex-DDR **MiG-21US** 24+06 is pictured at Peenemünde airfield on Germany's Baltic coast in May 2004.

Russia's first operational swept-wing jet fighter was the **MiG-15** (*Fagot*). More than 3,000 examples have been built and it has served with many former Warsaw Pact countries and third-world nations. '079 red' is in North Korean markings at the Military Museum in Beijing in December 1987. It features nine 'kill' markings.

For many air forces the MiG-15 was their first jet fighter, and a two-seat trainer was vital. This was the **MiG-15UTI** (*Midget*). Pictured, in June 1998, at the Hallinportti Museum in Finland is an ex-air force trainer MU-1.

Above: As the 'Iron Curtain' fell many MiGs were sold to private operators, especially in the USA. **MiG-15** N15PE is seen at an airshow at London, Ontario in June 1990.

Left: After the MiG-15 came the **MiG-17**. It entered service in the Soviet Union in the early 1950s. Known to NATO as *Fresco*, it was built in huge numbers – more than 8,000. '86 red' is in Bulgarian Air Force markings at the Warner Robins AFB Museum, Georgia in April 1994.

As well as the Russian production of the MiG-17, it was also built in Poland as the Lim-5. Many Polish examples had extensive modifications and more up-to-date equipment than the Russian ones. '634 blue' is in Soviet livery at the Pima County Museum, Arizona in October 1998. It is a Polish-built **Lim-5P** with nose radar.

Russian design bureau Lavochkin produced many fighters for the Soviet Air Force. Last of the line was the **La-250**. It was a very large two-seat, long-range, radar-equipped fighter armed with guided missiles. First flown in 1957, it did not go into production as it lost out to the Tu-128. '04 red' is at the Monino Museum in August 1995.

Below: Yakovlev built the first Russian VTOL aircraft. Unlike many such early projects, its powerplants, a pair of Tumanskii R11V turbojets, operated with rotary nozzles to give vectored thrust. **Yak-36** (*Freehand*) '36 red' is at the Monino Museum in August 1991.

An earlier Lavochkin design also failed to go into volume production. This was the **La-15** (*Fantail*). It was a swept-wing, single-seat fighter powered by an RD 500 turbojet of 3,500 lbst. This engine was a copy of the Rolls-Royce Derwent. The example seen here is in the Monino Museum in August 1991.

Yakovlev produced a whole family of twin-engined jets for the Russian military. The **Yak-25** (*Flashlight*) was a two-seat, radar-equipped, long-range fighter that entered service late in 1954. '80 red' is at the Central Air & Space Museum, Moscow in August 1995.

Above: Experience with the Yak-36 led to the production **Yak-38** (*Forger*). This type has seen operational service with the Russian Navy on board their aircraft carriers. The second prototype is pictured here in August 1991; it is to be found in the Yakovlev OKB Museum in Moscow.

Right: Seen in Russian Navy markings (note the flag on the intake) is **Yak-38M** '60 yellow'. With its wings folded and armed with unguided rocket pods, it is at the Central Air & Space Museum, Moscow in August 1991.

Known to NATO as *Mangrove*, the **Yak-27R** was a two-seat tactical reconnaissance machine powered by a pair of Tumanskii RD9AF turbojets giving a Mach 1.2 speed. '14 red' is at the Monino Museum in August 1991.

Above: The most radical development of the Yak-25 was the ultra-high-altitude reconnaissance variant. The wingspan was increased to 76ft 9in from the basic 36ft 1in. This version was designated **Yak-25RV** and known to NATO as *Mandrake*. The illustrated example is at the Monino Museum in August 1991.

Left: With a similar profile to the Yak-27 the **Yak-28R** was a supersonic light bomber capable of Mach 1.79 and known to NATO as *Brewer*. '91 black' is pictured at the Finow museum in Germany in May 2004.

Right: The first jet from the Yakovlev OKB was the **Yak-15** (*Feather*). This was a Yak-3 fitted with a Russian copy of the German-designed Junkers Jumo 004B engine. It flew from Zhukovsky for the first time on 24th April 1946 just a few hours after a MiG-9 had taken the honour of becoming the first Soviet jet at the same location. It had been decided who flew first by the flip of a coin! '37 yellow' is at the Yakovlev Museum, Moscow in August 1991.

Below: The next jet from Yakovlev was the **Yak-17** (also called *Feather*). The principal difference was the adoption of a nosewheel undercarriage. '02 blue' is at the Monino Museum in August 1991.

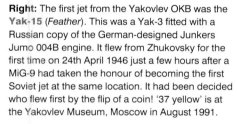

Power for the next production Yakovlev fighter came with the shipping to Russia of a number of Rolls-Royce Nene and Derwent engines in 1946 as a gift from the British government! These were quickly reverse-engineered and the **Yak-23** (*Flora*) was powered by a Derwent copy. '15 blue' is part of the Yak collection at the Monino Museum in August 1991.

The Soviet Union allowed Czechoslovakia, one of its satellite countries, to design and build its trainers. The **Aero L-29 Delfin** (*Maya*) was built in large numbers, approximately 3,600, and entered service in 1963. It has become a popular jet warbird for enthusiastic and rich pilots. N777ZE is pictured, in April 2005, at Lakeland, Florida.

Designed in Poland to meet the Warsaw Pact requirement for a basic/advanced jet trainer, the **PZL TS-11 Iskra** lost out to the Aero L-29. Poland decided to produce the type for its own air force and it was also sold to India. Examples have found their way to the private market in the USA. N718J is at an airshow at Lakeland, Florida in April 1994.

Left: Re-opened after the death of Stalin, the Sukhoi OKB's first jet was the **Su-7** (*Fitter*). Its main role was that of a ground-attack aircraft. '51' is an Su-7/S-26 fitted with skis for operations off snow, ice and unpaved runways. It is at the Monino Museum in August 1995.

Above left: The two-seat training variant of the *Fitter* is the **Su-7UM**, known to NATO as *Moujik*. The instructor, in the rear seat, has a periscope to give forward view. '16 red' is at the Central Air & Space Museum, Moscow in August 1995.

Above right: In 1959 the **Sukhoi Su-9** entered service with the Soviet Air Force in the role of an interceptor. It was a single-seat and -engined delta-wing craft. '10 red' is at Moscow's Central Air & Space Museum in August 1995.

Right: Known as *Fishpot* to NATO, the **Sukhoi Su-9** could carry four air-to-air missiles. The mounting pylons are visible under the wing of '68 blue' at Monino, Moscow in August 1991.

The next development from Sukhoi was the **Su-11**. This was based on the Su-9 but had uprated engines and better radar. It was given the NATO reporting name of *Fishpot-C*. '14 blue' is at the Monino Museum in August 1991.

Next in the Sukhoi line was the Su-15 (*Flagon*). This twin-engined interceptor was developed from the **Sukhoi T-58D-2** that first flew in 1963. This prototype is seen, in August 1995, at Monino.

Above: Two-seat Su-15s went into production in 1970, several years after the single-seat variants. As can be seen in the illustrated example, the field of view from the rear seat was not very good. **Sukhoi Su-15UT** '50 red' is at the Central Air & Space Museum, Moscow in August 1995.

Below: Pictured in October 2003, guarding the gate of the NCO Training School at the Peruvian Air Force Academy, Las Palmas, Lima is **Sukhoi Su-20** (*Fitter-F*) 005. This is an export version of the Su-17 and is incorrectly marked on the nose as an Su-22.

To improve the Su-7 in the ground-attack role, a new generation of Sukhoi fighters emerged based on the original airframe. The biggest difference was in the wings, which now had variable geometry, or swing-wings, from the outer part of the unit. **Su-17M-3** '93 red' (*Fitter-H*) is pictured, in August 1995, at Monino.

Above: Last of the *Fitter* line was the **Sukhoi Su-22M-4**. This had various upgrades of avionics and weapon loads. External changes included a ram-air inlet at the fin root. '757 red', a *Fitter-K*, is at the Luftfahrttechnischer Museumverein Rothenburg in the eastern part of Germany in May 2004.

Left: Sukhoi's Su-25 (*Frogfoot*) can be regarded as a jet follow-up to the World War Two (Great Patriotic War to the Russians) IL-2 Shturmovik. The concept was for an armoured ground-attack aircraft. First flown in 1975 it saw active service in Afghanistan. '301 black' is at the Central Air & Space Museum, Moscow in August 1995.

One of the most stylish and potent air-defence fighters to be found today is the **Sukhoi Su-27** (*Flanker*). A range of more than 2,000 miles, a Mach 2+ performance and high agility make it the current front-line Russian interceptor. '20 blue' is at the Central Air & Space Museum in August 1995.

A long-range low-level, all-weather bomber, the Sukhoi Su-24 (*Fencer*) replaced the IL -28 and Yak-28 in service. '61 yellow' was the **Sukhoi T-6-1** prototype for the series; first flown in 1967, it is pictured in August 1991 at the Monino Museum.

Left: The **Su-24** featured swing-wings. In addition to its bombing role it took on the tasks of tactical reconnaissance and electronic warfare. '54 red' is an early production aircraft pictured at Monino in August 1991.

Right: Few Mach 3 bombers have flown; in America there was the XB-70 and in Russia the **Sukhoi T-4**. It first flew in 1972 and made a total of only nine flights before the project was cancelled. '101 red' is pictured at Monino, Moscow, in August 1991, with the hinged nose in the down position. When this was up for high-speed flight the pilot had no forward vision at all and had to rely on instruments.

Below: Perhaps the most spectacular of all the Russian bombers was the **Myasishchev M-50** (*Bounder*). This four-engined supersonic bomber had an engine under each wing and another on each wingtip. Only one aircraft flew and this, '12 blue', is at the Monino Museum in August 1995.

First flown in 1948, the **Ilyushin IL-28** (*Beagle*) was a twin-engined, straight-wing, tactical bomber. It served in many roles and can still be found in service today in small numbers, as many were exported. '04 red' is at the Monino Museum in August 1991.

In the early 1950s, the Russians wanted a bomber capable of reaching the USA. The **Myasishchev M-4** (*Bison*) was built for this task. Production ran to only a few hundred and it was soon given a new role as a tanker and reconnaissance platform. '30 red' is at the Monino Museum in August 1991.

Not many airlines have high-altitude reconnaissance aircraft in their colours. Myasishchev produced the **M-17** (*Mystic*) with the probable intention of military service. The prototype, CCCP-17103, was operated in Aeroflot livery while doing earth survey work. It is pictured, in August 1991, at Monino.

The **Tupolev Tu-22** designation has been used for two different aircraft. The first was the *Blinder*, a supersonic bomber that flew in 1958. '81 red' is pictured, in August 1991, with Aeroflot training airframes at Moscow's Sheremetyevo Airport where it is supposed to have landed during an emergency and never left!

First variant of the *Backfire* in service was the **Tu-22M-2**. '48 red' is preserved among Aeroflot instructional airframes at Moscow-Sheremetyevo Airport in September 1995.

Above: The second Tupolev bomber with the designation was the **Tu-22M** (*Backfire*). This is a supersonic swing-wing strategic bomber and the current backbone of the Russian bomber fleet. '33 red' is one of the prototypes and is seen at Monino in August 1995.

Right: The most widely-used Russian bomber has to be the **Tupolev Tu-16** (*Badger*). A twin-engined machine, it has served in almost every role with the Russian Air Force and Navy as well as with export customers. '50 red' is at Monino in August 1991.

One of the later roles for the *Badger* was that of a launch platform for stand-off cruise missiles. '53 red', a **Tu-16K-26** at Monino in August 1995, has missiles under the wings.

A fighter bigger than most bombers, the **Tupolev Tu-128** was designed as a twin-engined, supersonic, missile-equipped interceptor with a very long range to counter attacks on Soviet airspace from any point. Known to NATO as *Fiddler* it has only in the past few years been replaced by MiG-31 and Su-27 aircraft. This example is at Monino in August 1995.

The **Kochyerigin DI-6** was a 1935 two-seat fighter. The rear gunner/observer sat behind the pilot to operate a gun. '3 white' is at the Central Museum of the Great Patriotic War in Moscow, in August 1995; and is thought to be the sole survivor of its type.

Polikarpov's **I-15** biplane fighter saw operational service during the Spanish Civil War as well as in the early part of World War Two. '50 white' is one of the indoor exhibits at Monino in August 1991.

Following the I-15 was the **Polikarpov I-16**, a stubby monoplane fighter with retractable undercarriage. It first flew in 1933. '51' is the only aircraft in the Navy Museum at St Petersburg, and is seen on display there in August 1991.

One of the rarest Russian aircraft to be found in any museum is the two-seat trainer **Polikarpov I-16UTI**. UT-1 is to be found at the Finnish Aviation Museum at Helsinki Airport, in June 1998. A number of Russian warplanes were captured during the 'Winter War' with Finland and pressed into service.

The **Ilyushin DB-3** (*Bob*) entered service in 1937. It was a twin-engined medium bomber that was developed and used throughout the war. '12' is at Monino in August 1991.

Left: At the start of the Great Patriotic War the **Tupolev SB-2** was the most important bomber in the Soviet Union, numerically speaking. However it suffered massive losses at the beginning of the conflict, as it was no match for the Bf 109s of the Luftwaffe. The illustrated example is at Monino in August 1995.

Below: The Lavochkin design bureau produced some of the finest of the Soviet piston-engined single-seat fighters. The **La-7** (*Fin*) was first flown in 1943, and was the mount of several of the highest-scoring Russian aces. '27 white' is an indoor exhibit at Monino in August 1991.

A three-crew, light tactical bomber, the **Petlyakov Pe-2** (*Buck*) was newly in service in June 1941 at the start of the German invasion of Russia. It remained in production throughout the war with more than 11,000 airframes being built. Pictured is the example at Monino in August 1991.

The **Lavochkin La-11** (*Fang*) looked very similar to the La-9. It was in fact a long-range version. One of the La-9's cannons was removed to make room for the extra fuel needed. 7505 is at the Beijing Aeronautical Institute in December 1987.

Above: Not flown until 1946, the **Lavochkin La-9** (*Fritz*) was an all-metal development of the La-5 and La-7. It was powered by a single ASh-82FN air-cooled radial piston engine of 1,850hp. 7504 is displayed at the Beijing Aeronautical Institute in December 1987.

Right: One of the earliest designs from the Sukhoi bureau was the **Su-2** light bomber. It was first flown in 1940 and served on many combat fronts. '27 white' is at the Central Museum of the Great Patriotic War, Moscow in August 1995.

Perhaps the most famous of all Russian aircraft of the Great Patriotic War period was the **Ilyushin IL-2 Shturmovik** (*Bark*). This was a heavily-armoured ground-attack machine with a single engine. '15 white' is displayed outside the Central Museum of the Great Patriotic War in August 1995.

Above: A fast medium bomber with twin ASh-82FN air-cooled radial piston engines of 1,850hp, the **Tupolev Tu-2** (*Bat*) was one of the most successful aircraft of the later war period. 44792 is a Chinese Air Force machine pictured at the Military Museum of China in central Beijing in December 1987.

Right: The first production units of the IL-2 were single-seat. These proved to be vulnerable to attack from the rear by German fighters. It was decided to produce a two-seater with a gunner to cover the previous blind spot. This example of an **IL-2-M3** is pictured outside the Ilyushin OKB facility in Moscow in August 1991.

The IL-10 was exported to a number of communist states. When it was in service there was a need for a training aircraft. This was produced as the **IL-10UTI**, the main differences being the lack of fixed armament and the shape of the rear canopy. '10 white' is a Chinese Air Force example at the China Aviation Museum in October 1999.

Above: The design bureau produced an improved Shturmovik in the shape of the **IL-10** (*Beast*). It was slightly smaller but had a 2,000hp AM 42 liquid-cooled piston engine. It entered service in the early months of 1945 and was a great improvement over its predecessor. This example is at the Monino Museum in August 1991.

Right: Mitsubishi in Japan produced, with some input from Germany, the **J8M1 Shusui** (*Sword Stroke*). This was a copy of the Me 163 rocket-powered fighter. It had reached flight trials when the war ended. 403 is pictured at the Planes of Fame Museum at Chino, California in October 1984.

Right: Another Japanese 'copy' of a German design was the **Nakajima Kikka** (Orange Blossom). The aircraft was externally similar to the Me 262 but of smaller dimensions. The first aircraft flew on 7th August 1945, only a week before the end of hostilities. 91-ST is pictured at the Paul Garber Facility of the Smithsonian Institute at Silver Hill, Maryland in May 1989.

Below: A long-range, twin-engined escort or night fighter the **Nakajima J1N1-S Gekko** (Moonlight) had a pair of fuselage-mounted 20mm cannons that fired upwards. The aircraft could fly under its prey and destroy it without being seen. 7334 is at Silver Hill in May 1989. It has since moved to the new site at Washington-Dulles Airport.

Above: Floatplane fighters have never been a common sight. Such a machine was the **Kawanishi N1K1 Kyofu** (Mighty Wind). Its role was to support offensive operations where no airfields were available. 565 is pictured at NAS Willow Grove, Pennsylvania in May 1989.

Above: Most famous of all the World War Two Japanese aircraft is the **Mitsubishi A6M Reisen** (Zero) which fought from the start of the Pacific War through to the end. A6M3 Y2-128 is pictured, in October 2004, at the Air & Space Museum in the Nagoya Airport terminal building. This airframe was recovered from a jungle crash site and restored to its original condition.

Below: Most numerous of the Japanese Army fighters throughout the war was the **Nakajima Ki-43 Hayabusa** (Peregrine Falcon). This example, c/n 6430, is at the Experimental Aircraft Association Museum at Oshkosh, Wisconsin in August 1986.

Above: While Kawanishi was working on the floatplane fighter it also proposed a land-based version. This was the **N1K2-J Shiden Kai**. 343-35 is pictured when at the Champlin Fighter Museum, Mesa, Arizona in October 1998.

Below: One of the few Japanese fighters with a liquid-cooled engine was the **Kawasaki Ki-61 Hien** (Swallow). The example shown was being restored at Chino, California, in October 1984. it is believed to have been recovered from an island in the Pacific. It has now moved to the care of the Fantasy of Flight Museum at Polk City, Florida.

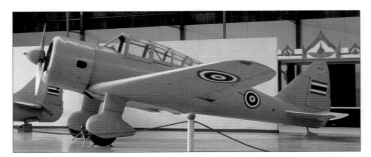

In 1937 a specification was issued in Japan for a two-seat army co-operation aircraft with rough-field capability. First flown the following year, the **Tachikawa Ki-36** was powered by a single 450hp Hitachi Ha13 air-cooled radial piston engine. The sole surviving example is seen at the Royal Thai Air Force Museum, Bangkok in November 1989.

Above: Kawasaki's Ki-100 was produced as a direct result of the need for an interceptor to counter the formations of B-29s at 30,000ft. The short-term solution was to fit a 1,500hp Mitsubishi HA-112 radial engine to the airframe of the Ki-61. The resultant Ki-100 was one of the best fighters the Japanese Army had. 8476M is at the RAF Museum Cosford in May 1989.

Left: The Ki-36 proved to be an ideal airframe to train pilots, and many were converted to this role. All unnecessary equipment was removed to save weight, including the wheel spats. Such conversions were redesignated **Tachikawa Ki-55**. 02 is pictured, in December 1987, at the Military Museum of China, Beijing.

One of the more elegant aircraft designs from Japan was the **Mitsubishi Ki-46**. It was a twin-engined, two-seat, photo-reconnaissance aircraft. It had a range of more than 2,000 miles and a service ceiling of 36,000ft. 5439/8484M is at the RAF Museum Cosford in August 1994.

Above: Few Japanese bombers of World War Two have survived. Seen at the China Aviation Museum, in October 1999, is **Kawasaki Ki-48** 308. This was a twin-engined light bomber with a crew of four. Many of the aircraft were used in the final stages of the Pacific War as suicide bombers.

Right: Designed by the team that produced the A6M Zero, the **Mitsubishi J2M Raiden** (Thunderbolt) was beset with technical problems and never achieved the planned volume production. However units that operated it found it to be a formidable fighter. 91-101 is pictured, in October 1979, as part of the Planes of Fame collection at Chino, California.

When the film *Tora! Tora! Tora!* was made, the producers needed a supply of Japanese fighters together with dive- and torpedo-bombers in flying condition. Since no originals were available they made realistic replicas. N3725G is a **Nakajima B5N** torpedo-bomber. It is part of the then Confederate Air Force and is seen at Harlingen, Texas in October 1979.

A Vultee Valiant was the basis for this replica of an **Aichi D3A** dive-bomber. N56336 is seen at an airshow at Biggs AAF base, El Paso, Texas in October 1984.

Built from non-strategic materials, the **Heinkel He 162** was a single-seat jet fighter that entered service in the last months of World War Two. It was powered by a single BMW 003 turbojet of 1,760 lbst. 120227/8472M is pictured at St Athan in September 1983; it is now at the RAF Museum, Hendon.

The **Messerschmitt Me 163B Komet** was the world's first operational rocket-powered interceptor. It had a very short range, only about ten minutes at full speed, but was able to climb to 30,000ft inside three. 191904 is pictured at the Luftwaffe Museum, Gatow, Berlin in May 2004.

Perhaps the best-known World War Two jet was the **Messerschmitt Me 262**. It is fortunate for the Allies that it was not put into front-line service as early as it could have been. Hitler's demands that it be used as a bomber kept it back for many months and by the time it saw action it was too late to have an effect. 112372/8482M, seen here in May 1989, was part of the RAF Museum at Cosford.

Since the **Me 262** was a totally new concept to the pilots, a two-seater trainer was produced. Other two-place aircraft were used as radar-equipped night fighters. Me 262B 110639 is at Willow Grove NAS, Pennsylvania in May 1989. It has since moved to the Victory Air Museum in New Jersey.

First flown in 1936, the **Messerschmitt Bf 110** was a twin-engined, two-seat fighter and fighter-bomber. Power was supplied by a pair of Daimler-Benz DB605 liquid-cooled piston engines of 1,475hp each. It was used throughout World War Two on all fronts. 730301/8479M is at the RAF Museum, Hendon in November 1986.

The **Messerschmitt Me 410** was not one of the more successful projects from the company. It developed out of the Me 210 and was used as a night-fighter and fighter-bomber. 420430/8483M is at the RAF Museum Cosford in May 1983.

The **Junkers Ju 88** was the Luftwaffe's most versatile aircraft It was a high-speed medium bomber as well as a formidable radar-equipped night fighter. First flown in 1936, it served throughout the war. 360043/8475M is at the RAF Museum, Hendon in October 1986.

The main use of the **Dornier Do 24T** was for air-sea rescue. A flying-boat, it was powered by three BMW-Bramo 323R air-cooled radial piston engines of 1,000hp. The last service use of the type was by the Spanish Air Force who flew them from Majorca into the 1960s. HD.5-2 is pictured at the Museo del Aire at Cuatro Vientos, Madrid in September 2002.

The reconnaissance and anti-submarine **Arado Ar 196** floatplane was the standard catapult aircraft of the German Navy. It was powered by a single BMW 132K air-cooled radial piston engine of 900hp. 623183/T3+HK is seen at Willow Grove NAS, Pennsylvania in May 1989. This aircraft once served on the battle-cruiser *Prinz Eugen*.

Above left: The name Stuka commonly given to the **Junkers Ju 87** is derived from the word 'Sturzkampfflugzeug' (dive-bomber). The two-seater was an effective bomber and ground-attack aircraft but was slow and cumbersome against fighter attack. 494083/8474M is seen at RAF Chivenor in August 1970; it is now to be found at the RAF Museum Hendon.

Above right: The **Arado Ar 234 Blitz** (Lightning) was the world's first jet bomber. Power came from a pair of Junkers Jumo 004B turbojets of 1,980 lbst each. It did not commence operations until the start of 1945, too late to make a difference. 140312 is an immaculate restoration pictured when at Silver Hill, Maryland in May 1989.

Left: One of the most widely-used torpedo-bombers of World War Two, the **Grumman TBM Avenger** was a carrier-borne aircraft with a crew of three and was powered by a single Wright R-2600 radial piston engine of 1,850hp. N3966A/53319 (now G-BTDP) is privately-owned and is seen flying at Old Warden, Bedfordshire in July 1989.

Left: Canada was home to the last 'operational' **Avengers**. They could be found in New Brunswick protecting forests in their role as water-bombers until the recent past. C-GCWG/91450 was part of the Canadian Warplane Heritage and is seen at its Hamilton, Ontario base in June 1990. In February 1993 it was destroyed in a hangar fire.

Below left: The combination of an Italian airframe and a German engine produced one of the better fighters to equip squadrons of the Regia Aeronautica from 1941. The aircraft was the **Macchi C202 Folgore** (Thunderbolt) and the powerplant was the DB601A liquid-cooled piston engine of 1,200hp licence-built in Italy. MM9476 is seen on display at the NASM, Washington DC in May 1989.

Below right: For the Soviet Air Force in World War Two the **Yakovlev Yak-9** was the most widely-produced and important single-seat fighter. Nearly 17,000 came off the production line. The illustrated example here is at the Army & Military Museum in Kiev, Ukraine in August 1991.

Above left: The ultimate basic type of **Yak-9** was the 'U' (*Uluchshennyi* or improved). '36 white' is at the Champlin Fighter Museum at Mesa, Arizona in October 1998.

Above right: Despite the difference in their designations the **Yakovlev Yak-3** followed on from the Yak-9. Nearly 4,000 airframes were produced. It was used as both a fighter and ground-attack aircraft. '4' is pictured, in July 1970, in the Musée de l'Air in Paris.

Right: In what is one of the most amazing come-back stories, the Yak-3 was returned to production in 1991 by the Yakovlev company to satisfy demand from American collectors for flying warbirds. Since they are made by the same company, they can be classed as real Yak-3s, with just a fifty-year gap in the line! Power for the 'new' aircraft is an Allison V-1710 liquid-cooled piston engine of 1,240hp. **Yak 3UA** c/n 07040101 was the prototype and is seen at Zhukovsky in August 1995.

Tigercats are flown by a number of lucky warbird owners. Their use as water-bombers to fight forest fires until the early 1980s ensured an available stock of airframes. F7F-3 NX700F is at the EAA fly-in at Oshkosh, Wisconsin in July 1986.

Above: A carrier-based fighter-bomber, the twin-engined **Grumman F7F Tigercat** was powered by a pair of P&W R-2800 air-cooled radial piston engines of 2,100hp each. This gave a maximum speed of 435mph. F7F-3 80373 is in USMC markings at the US Navy Museum, Pensacola in April 1994.

Left: North American's **F-82 Twin Mustang** was born of the need for a long-range fighter for the Pacific war. Two P-51H fuselages with modified wings were put together. It was too late for World War Two but saw action in Korea as a night fighter. N1210Z is with the then Confederate Air Force at Harlingen, Texas in October 1979.

Right: Australia produced the **Commonwealth CA-12 Boomerang** using components from the Wirraway trainer. With the Japanese advance in the Pacific in late 1941 the RAAF was short of fighters. It says much for the capabilities of the Australians that the prototype first flew in May 1942. Production was 250 airframes and it saw operational service in ground attack, army co-operation and reconnaissance roles. Pictured in February 2003 at the RAAF Museum, Point Cook, Victoria is Boomerang 1 A46-30.

Below: 'Second to none' is the cry from the crews of the **Handley Page Halifax** heavy bomber of World War Two. The aircraft always suffered from being overshadowed by the Lancaster in the history of the bomber offensive. As the 1970s dawned there was not a Halifax to be found as post-war aircraft preservation policy had been to scrap everything that had flown! One was found in a Norwegian lake and recovered 'as is' to the RAF Museum. Illustrated, in July 1997, is Halifax II LV907 rebuilt by the Yorkshire Aircraft Museum at Elvington from the remains of several aircraft. Yorkshire was the home of most of Bomber Command's Halifax squadrons.

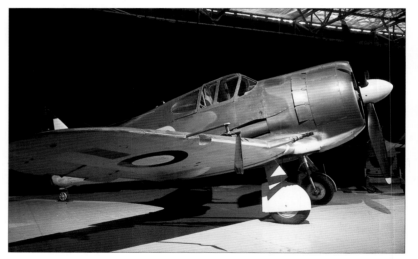

First flown in 1936, the Fieseler Fi 156 Storch (Stork) had an amazing short-field performance for its day. It served throughout the war in a communications and light-transport role. Morane-Saulnier in France produced the Storch under occupation. Since it was a very good design, production continued after 1945 for the French military as the **MS.500**. As the warbird movement became popular German markings were often applied. Privately-owned MS.500/Fi 156 N40FS is seen at the Gathering of the Warbirds show at Madera, California in August 1986.

The RCAF Memorial Museum at Trenton, Ontario, has restored **Halifax VII** NA337, which was hit by flak whilst on a mission to drop supplies to the Norwegian resistance in April 1945 and ditched in Lake Mjosa with only one survivor. Fifty years later it was raised and taken to Canada for re-building. The aircraft is pictured in September 2005, just prior to being painted.

Consolidated's PBY Catalina first flew in 1935 and went on to be the most widely produced flying-boat ever. As well as US Navy and RAF service in World War Two the Catalina served with many air forces and navies around the world post 1945. FAE 1665 PBY-5A is pictured, in September 1997, at the Ecuadorian Air Force Museum at Quito.

This **Catalina** is an ex-Canadian water-bomber, having been operated by Flying Fireman from Vancouver Island. It is pictured, in September 2002, at the Museo Del Aire in Madrid. A PBY-5A, it carries the Spanish military serial of DR.1/74-21.

Above: For the American public, World War Two is summed up by the **Boeing B-17 Flying Fortress**. It was in service for the whole of the conflict and served in secondary roles long after. N9323Z/44-83514 flies as *Sentimental Journey*. Owned by the then Confederate Air Force, it is pictured arriving at the Gathering of the Warbirds show at Madera, California in August 1986.

Left: Now owned by the Vintage Flying Museum at Fort Worth, Texas, **Boeing B-17G** N3701G/44-8543 flies as *Chuckie*. It is seen in August 1986, at the EAA fly-in at Oshkosh, Wisconsin.

An ex-US Navy PB-1W, this **B-17G** N5233V/44-83863 is pictured in October 1981 as part of the USAF Armament Museum at Eglin AFB, Florida.

Offutt AFB, Nebraska, was home to the Strategic Air Command, which operated the USAF's bomber fleets. It is fitting that there is a **B-17G** in its museum. 44-83559 is marked, in July 1986, as 23474 and *King Bee*.

61

Left: In France the Institut Géographique National at Creil flew the **B-17G** on survey work into the 1970s. G-BEDF/44-85784 is from this stock. It flies the UK airshow circuit as *Sally B* and is pictured at North Weald in May 1989.

Below: Another former French IGN **Boeing B-17G**, F-BDRS/44-83735, is pictured in May 1996 as part of the Imperial War Museum collection at Duxford. It is displayed as 231983 *Mary Alice*.

When B-17s were severely damaged over Germany and could not make it back to the UK, the crews of some tried to get to neutral Switzerland rather than become prisoners-of-war. **B-17G** 42-38160 landed in Lake Zug and was recovered in 1952. It was displayed in a number of locations and is pictured, in July 1970, at St Moritz marked as *Lonesome Polecat*. It was scrapped in 1972.

Pictured in October 1984, is one of the longest continually-displayed **Flying Fortresses**, 44-85738 DB-17G (a post-war USAF drone director). It has been in the charge of the American Veterans of Foreign Wars at Tulare, California, since 1958.

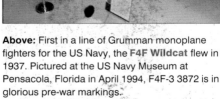

Above: First in a line of Grumman monoplane fighters for the US Navy, the **F4F Wildcat** flew in 1937. Pictured at the US Navy Museum at Pensacola, Florida in April 1994, F4F-3 3872 is in glorious pre-war markings.

Right: Since vast numbers of aircraft were required during World War Two, many were produced by other manufactures to meet demand. General Motors built the **Wildcat** under the designation FM-2. N6209C is a privately-owned warbird and is seen at the EAA fly-in at Oshkosh, Wisconsin in August 1996.

Left: Second of the Grumman single-engine, single-seat fighters for the US Navy was the **F6F Hellcat**. It was the most important of all the Navy's World War Two fighters. First flown in 1942, it entered service the following year. F6F-5K NX4PP is a privately-owned warbird at Oshkosh in August 1986.

Below left: When **Hellcat** production ended in 1945, more than 12,000 airframes had been built. F6F-5K G-BTCC/40467 is a British-based warbird seen landing at its Duxford base in July 1997.

Below right: Last of the Grumman single-engined, piston-powered fighters for the US Navy was the **F8F Bearcat**. Too late for World War Two, it saw action with the French in Indo-China. F8F-2P NX700HL is a British-based warbird about to take off at Duxford in July 1991.

Above left: The Royal Thai Air Force operated **Bearcats** during the 1950s. F8F-1 15-178/98 is pictured, in November 1999, in the service's Bangkok museum.

Above right: Two civil variants of the **Bearcat** were made under the designation G-58. One was for Gulf Oil and the other retained by the manufacturer as company demonstrator N700A. The latter is seen as part of the Champlin Fighter Museum at Mesa, Arizona, in October 1984. It is now part of the Palm Springs Museum in California.

Right: The most drastic modifications to a **Bearcat** are those of the Unlimited racer, the fastest motor-sport in the world. N777L F8F-2 is named *Rare Bear* and is seen in September 1988 at Reno, Nevada – the winner of that year's 'Gold Race'.

A unique layout in the **Bell P-39 Airacobra** had the engine positioned behind the pilot in the fuselage. First flown in 1939, it was not as well regarded as other contemporary fighters. However half the production went to Russia under Lend-Lease. N40A is a privately-owned warbird and is seen visiting the CAF show at Harlingen, Texas in October 1979.

A direct development of the P-39 was the **P-63 Kingcobra**. As with the earlier model most went to Russia, with France receiving a number post-war. G-BTWR/42-69097 is in private hands and is pictured at its Duxford base in July 1994.

The principal carrier-based dive-bomber for the US Navy for most of World War Two was the **Douglas SBD Dauntless**. N54532, operated by the Confederate Air Force, is seen at the CAF's then Harlingen, Texas base in October 1979.

The **Curtiss P-40 Warhawk/Tomahawk** was to be found on almost every front during World War Two. In the USA its volume production was topped only by the P-51 and P-47. Privately-owned warbird NL1009N P-40N is pictured in June 1985 at RAF Coningsby in the famous sharks-teeth markings pioneered by 112 Squadron RAF in the North African campaign.

Above left: *Burma Rascal* is the name of this dramatically-marked **Curtiss P-40** N293FR. It is seen visiting Oshkosh, Wisconsin in August 1986.

Above right: Built by Douglas, the **A-20 Havoc** was a light bomber powered by a pair of Wright R-2600 radial pistons. N3WF is pictured visiting an airshow at Biggs AAF Base, El Paso, in October 1984. It is now preserved at the Lone Star Flight Museum, Galveston, Texas.

Left: Pictured, in August 1995, at the Monino Museum, Moscow, is **Douglas A-20 Havoc** 43-10052. The type was delivered to the Russians under Lend-Lease.

Right: One of the most important British warplanes of all time was the **Hawker Hurricane**. In the Battle of Britain it shot down more enemy aircraft than its contemporary, the headline-grabbing Spitfire. LF363 is still operated by the RAF as part of the Battle of Britain Memorial Flight. It is pictured when in the markings of 85 Squadron as a night fighter, at its home base of Coningsby in June 1986.

Below left: Belgium was a pre-war operator of the **Hawker Hurricane**. Pictured in June 1983 in RAF markings at the Royal Army Museum in Brussels, LF658 is marked as 'LF345'.

Below right: It is fitting that the last-ever **Hurricane** built should be preserved. PZ865 is pictured at an airshow at RAF Fairford in July 1989. It is operated by the RAF's Battle of Britain Memorial Flight.

Above left: Hurricanes were manufactured in Canada by Canadian Car & Foundry Ltd. C-GCWH/P3069 is one such aircraft. It is seen operated by the Canadian Warplane Heritage Museum at Hamilton, Ontario in June 1990. Sadly it was destroyed in a hangar fire in 1993.

Above right: 5418 is a Canadian-built **Hurricane XII** and is on show at the Reynolds Aviation Museum in Alberta in May 2000.

Left: The **Sea Hurricane**, used in small numbers, was fitted with a tail-hook and catapult spools. G-BKTH/Z7015 is owned by the Shuttleworth Trust and seen at Duxford in May 1996.

1935 saw the first variant of what was to become the most widely-used trainer ever. This was the **North American NA-64/BT-9 Yale**. C-GCWY/3350 is pictured in June 1990 with the Canadian Warplane Heritage Museum at Hamilton, Ontario.

Above: With the same basic layout as the Yale but with a 600hp P&W R-1340 engine in place of the 400hp Wright R-975 and a retractable undercarriage, the **North American T-6 Harvard/Texan** became the advanced trainer of the free world. It remained in service with the South African Air Force until the early 1990s. MM54098 T-6G is pictured, in September 2004, preserved at the Italian Air Force base of Grazzanise.

Left: Many of the air forces of the world that operated the **Harvard** have preserved examples. Seen here is one at the Royal Thai Air Force Museum at Bangkok in November 1999.

Preserved within the military area at Quito Airport in September 1997, is FAE 43233 **AT-6C Harvard** of the Ecuadorian Air Force.

Above: This Venezuelan example of the **Harvard**, 2175, is pictured in November 1992 on a traffic roundabout in the city of Maracay.

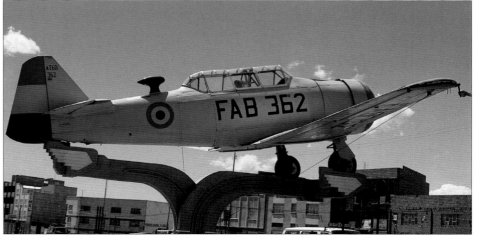

Left: Pictured, in November 1992, at the gate of air force headquarters at La Paz Airport, Bolivia, is **AT-6D Harvard** FAB 362.

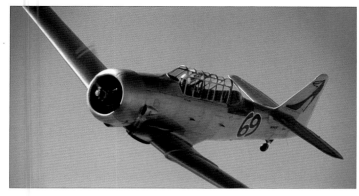

With the numbers available and its relatively attractive running costs, the **Harvard** has become a very popular private warbird. At the Reno Air Races, the Harvard competitions are the closest as they are all stock aircraft. N6424D is seen rounding a pylon in September 1988.

Pictured in October 2003 on the parade ground of Uruguay's basic training base, Pando, is **North American T-6 Texan** 340.

Above left: N662DB is a **Super T-6** and has a new powerplant; note the three-bladed propeller and redesigned rudder. It is seen at the EAA fly-in at Lakeland, Florida in April 1994.

Above right: The **Harvard** can make a very good double for the Japanese Zero fighter. A number were converted in 1968 for the Hollywood film *Tora! Tora! Tora!*. These proved to be popular warbirds. N7757 is one such conversion and is pictured in September 1988 at Sonoma Valley, California.

Right: The Supermarine Spitfire was in front-line service as a fighter from the beginning of World War Two until the end. Its development stretched from the Mk I with a 1,030hp Rolls-Royce Merlin to the 2,050hp Griffon in the F.24. **Spitfire II** P7350 is still operated by the RAF as part of the BBMF. It is pictured at its Coningsby base in June 1986.

Owned by the Shuttleworth Trust, **Spitfire V** G-AWII/AR501 is pictured at its Old Warden base in July 1989.

A popular warbird on the airshow circuit is **Spitfire IX** G-ASJV/MH343. It is pictured at Liverpool-Speke in August 1984.

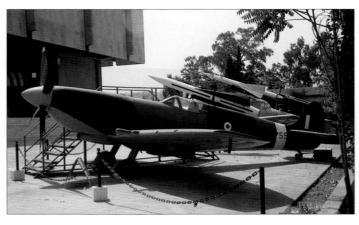

Delivered to the Greek Air Force in 1947, **Spitfire IX** MJ775 is seen in June 1993, displayed at the Hellenic War Museum in Athens.

Operated in Australia **Spitfire HF.VIII** VH-HET/ A58-602 is pictured, in February 2003, about to take off for a display at Avalon. It carries the livery representing a Spitfire of 457 squadron flown by Australian ace Wing Commander R H (Bobby) Gibbes in 1945.

Originally operated by the Irish Air Corps as a two-seat trainer, this **Spitfire T.9** is now based in the USA. N308WK/TE308 is pictured on a visit to Oshkosh in August 1986.

Most **Spitfires** are operated in military markings so it was a refreshing change to see Mk XIV G-FIRE in an all-red livery as a privately-owned aircraft. It has since been sold in the USA and has adopted a camouflage scheme. It is seen at Mildenhall in May 1981.

Above left: One of many post-war operators of the **Spitfire**, the Royal Thai Air Force has preserved this example. Mk XIV 14-1/93 is at its museum in Bangkok in November 1999.

Above right: With an appropriate registration **Spitfire XIV** G-SPIT/MV293 is one of a growing number of airworthy UK-based machines. It is seen at its Duxford base in May 1996.

Left: The market for flying Spitfires grows. Many aircraft have been restored to flying condition from what would have been regarded as scrap airframes only twenty years ago. **Spitfire XVIII** G-BTXE/TP280 is pictured at Duxford, in July 1992, following a full restoration. It now flies in the USA as N280TP.

The last service use, as opposed to ceremonial use, of the Spitfire with the RAF was with the THUM (Temperature & Humidity) Flight at RAF Woodvale. All three aircraft that were used still survive. Seen at West Malling, in August 1989, at an airshow is one of them, **Spitfire PR.XIX** PS853, being operated by the BBMF. It has since been sold to Rolls-Royce and re-registered as G-RRGN.

Above: There are now far more flying Spitfires than forty years ago. **Spitfire PR.XI** G-MKXI/PL965 is pictured displaying at Duxford in July 1997.

Left: For many years Spitfires were used as gate guards at RAF stations. Most have been rescued and some restored to flying condition; others are stored. **Spitfire 22** PK664/7759M is on the gate at RAF Binbrook in September 1977. Following the closure of the base it went into storage at RAF Cardington and later to the RAF Museum Restoration Centre at Cosford.

Below: Supermarine produced a naval version of its most famous craft as the Seafire. As can be seen in this picture the wings folded, as did the wingtips. **Seafire XVII** SX137 is at the Fleet Air Arm Museum at Yeovilton in December 1977.

Above: Last of the direct line was the **Spitfire 24**. VN485/7326M is seen in July 1991 as part of the Imperial War Museum collection at Duxford.

Right: Final development of the whole Spitfire/Seafire range was the Rolls-Royce Griffon-engined **Seafire F.47** with a contra-rotating propeller. This device eliminated the torque effect of the single prop. VP441 is pictured in store at Lavenham in October 1969. After a lengthy rebuild in Texas it now flies in Montana.

One of the largest single-seat, single-engined fighters of World War Two was the **Republic P-47 Thunderbolt**. More than 15,000 were produced and it served on many fronts. Service continued with Air National Guard units until as late as 1955. A number of South American air forces received the type, FAC 861 is seen with the Colombian Air Force Museum at Bogotá in November 1992.

With a non-standard tailwheel, **P-47D** 450 is a Peruvian example at the air force museum at Las Palmas, Lima in September 1997. This airframe has since been sold to a warbird-collector in the USA and moved to Arizona.

P-47D Thunderbolt 10B36 is in the Venezuelan Air Force Museum at Maracay in November 1992.

Some of the airworthy **P-47 Thunderbolts** in the USA are ex-South American aircraft. NX14519, pictured in October 1984 at the Champlin Fighter Museum, Mesa, Arizona, is an ex-Bolivian machine. It carries the name *Big Stud*. Along with many other aircraft from the Champlin collection, it is now in the Personal Courage Wing of the Museum of Flight at Boeing Field.

Left: Owned by the Lone Star Flight Museum at Galveston, Texas, **P-47G Thunderbolt** N47DG is seen marked as *Little Demon* at Oshkosh in August 1986.

Below: An observation and scout aircraft, the **Vought OS2U Kingfisher** served the US Navy from 1940; it also had limited export sales. OS2U-3 314 is in Chilean Air Force colours at the Museo Nacional de Aeronautica de Chile at Los Cerrillos, Santiago, in October 2004. This airframe flew in the Chilean Antarctic region during the late 1940s.

A restoration project awaiting the person with sufficient time and dollars to deal with the Chinese government, **P-47D Thunderbolt** 7601 is seen at the Beijing Aeronautical Institute in December 1987.

Above left: Built in very large numbers, the **Messerschmitt Bf 109** was the best-known fighter used by the Luftwaffe during World War Two. The Swiss Air Force was one of the few export recipients of the type. Bf 109E J-355 is pictured, in September 2004, at their museum at Dubendorf.

Above right: During its brief flying career **Bf 109G** G-USTV/10639 was the only authentic aircraft from the days of the Axis powers left in the air. Owned by the Imperial War Museum it is seen flying at its Duxford base in July 1997. It is now in the RAF Museum at Hendon following restoration after a crash-landing in October 1997.

Left: Finland was another operator of the **Bf 109G**. MT-507 is on display at the air force museum at Tikkakoski in June 1998.

Above left: When the Spanish Air Force put the Bf 109 into licensed production after World War Two it incorporated the Rolls-Royce Merlin to power the aircraft. **Hispano HA-1112 Buchon** C4K-156 is on display at the Musée de l'Air in May 1983.

Above right: Spain operated the **HA-1112 Buchon** until the mid-1960s and many have found their way into the warbird market. They are usually painted in German markings; G-HUNN is privately-owned and seen here at Duxford in July 1989.

Right: Renowned as a radar-equipped night-fighter and a torpedo-bomber for Coastal Command, the **Bristol Beaufighter** served the RAF as late as 1960 as a target-tug out in the Far East. RD867, a TT.10, is pictured at RAF Abingdon in June 1968. The aircraft is now part of the National Aviation Museum of Canada in Ottawa.

One of the Fleet Air Arm's most famous aircraft, with many battle honours, was the **Fairey Swordfish**. Its main role was as a carrier-based torpedo-bomber. LS326 is operated by the Royal Navy Historic Flight and is seen at Cranfield in July 1987.

Above: The **Vought F4U Corsair** was the finest of all the US Navy's single-seat fighters of World War Two. It was still in service during the Korean War. F4U-7 NX1337P/133722 is in French Navy markings at Duxford in July 1992. Privately-owned, it has since been sold in the USA.

Left: Inverted gull-wings to keep the undercarriage short while still allowing a powerful engine are the recognisable features of the design. **F4U-5N Corsair** N49068/124453 is a privately-owned warbird and is pictured at Mojave, California in September 1988.

Right: Goodyear produced **Corsairs** with the designation FG-1. N8297/88297 (now G-FGID) is operated from Duxford where it is seen landing in July 1991.

Below: Power was increased in the **Corsair** with the introduction of water-methanol injection. This enabled it to produce 2,450hp. The prototype of this variant was the XF4U-4. 80759 is seen in July 1986 on display at the New England Air Museum, Connecticut.

In US Marine Corps markings is **FG-1D Corsair** 92085. It is pictured at the Selfridge ANG base, Michigan in June 1990.

The big engine power of the **F2G Corsair** led to one of the airframes being converted to a 'Super Corsair' for Unlimited racing. N31518 is pictured at the Reno Races in September 1988.

Goodyear developed a low-altitude version of the **Corsair** for the USMC. Power was supplied by a P&W R-4360. It did not go into production. F2G-1 Corsair N4324/88454 is displayed at the Champlin Fighter Museum in October 1984.

Built as an army co-operation aircraft, the **Westland Lysander** played a vital role in World War Two thanks to its short take-off and landing performance. This was the task of transporting agents into enemy-occupied Europe. OO-SOT/2442 Lysander IIIA is seen flying at RAF Fairford in July 1995. It is operated by the Sabena Old Timers Foundation in Belgium.

The **Westland Lysander** was built under licence in Canada. One of its roles was that of a target-tug. C-GCWL/2363 is seen wearing the very high visibility marking associated with this task. It is owned by the Canadian Warplane Heritage at Hamilton, Ontario, where it is pictured in September 2005.

A three-crew night fighter, the **Northrop P-61 Black Widow** first flew in 1942. Its first kill was in July 1944 in the Pacific where it had been introduced into service. 7602 is one of only four airframes believed to be complete. It is at the Beijing Aeronautical Institute in December 1987.

An amphibian with a pusher propeller, the **Supermarine Seagull V** first flew in 1933. It saw service as a catapult-launched navy spotter in the Fleet Air Arm, who gave it the name Walrus. Pictured, in February 2003, at the Royal Australian Air Force Museum at Point Cook is Walrus II HD874 resplendent in an all-yellow colour scheme.

The **Supermarine Walrus** found fame in a new role during World War Two as an air-sea rescue craft plucking many downed pilots from the sea. L2301 is seen at the FAA Museum at Yeovilton in July 1985.

Left: A two-crew, carrier-based bomber, the **Curtiss SB2C Helldiver** first saw operational service in 1943. 83479 is pictured in April 1994, at the US Navy Museum at Pensacola, Florida.

Below: The Royal Thai Air Force was another operator of the **Curtiss Helldiver**. SB2C-5 83410 is pictured, in November 1989, in Bangkok.

Helldivers were supplied to a number of nations that did not have aircraft carriers. SB2C-5 83321 is at the Hellenic War Museum, Athens, in June 1993, wearing Greek Air Force markings.

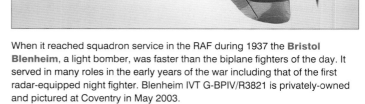

When it reached squadron service in the RAF during 1937 the **Bristol Blenheim**, a light bomber, was faster than the biplane fighters of the day. It served in many roles in the early years of the war including that of the first radar-equipped night fighter. Blenheim IVT G-BPIV/R3821 is privately-owned and pictured at Coventry in May 2003.

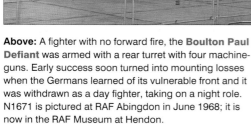

Above: A fighter with no forward fire, the **Boulton Paul Defiant** was armed with a rear turret with four machine-guns. Early success soon turned into mounting losses when the Germans learned of its vulnerable front and it was withdrawn as a day fighter, taking on a night role. N1671 is pictured at RAF Abingdon in June 1968; it is now in the RAF Museum at Hendon.

Right: Designed by Kurt Tank, the **Focke-Wulf Fw 190** was introduced into service during late 1941. It immediately proved to be the best fighter of that time. Power was from a BMW 801 radial piston engine of 1,660hp. Fw 190A-8 733682 is displayed at the Imperial War Museum in London in February 1990.

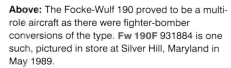

Considered to be the finest piston-engined aircraft produced by Germany, the long-nosed **Focke-Wulf Fw 190D** was powered by a liquid-cooled Junkers Jumo 213. NX190D is pictured when with the Champlin Fighter Museum in October 1998.

Above: The Focke-Wulf 190 proved to be a multi-role aircraft as there were fighter-bomber conversions of the type. **Fw 190F** 931884 is one such, pictured in store at Silver Hill, Maryland in May 1989.

Right: Spain used the **CASA 2-111** until the late 1960s; they featured in the film *Battle of Britain* and were then sold to collectors and museums. N72615 is part of the Confederate Air Force and, until a fatal crash in July 2003, was operated by the Arizona Wing from Mesa. It is pictured there in October 1998.

Designed for the role of a fighter and reconnaissance aircraft for the Navy, the **Fairey Firefly** first flew in 1941. Power was from a Rolls-Royce Griffon. Firefly FR.1 SF11 is a Thai example in the museum in Bangkok in November 1999.

Above: Pictured, in September 2002, at Spain's Museo del Aire is B.2-82, a genuine German-built **Heinkel He 111E**. This aircraft served in the Spanish Civil War and is the only example of its type remaining in the world. Note the nose is a different configuration from later variants. Spain licence-built the He 111 as the CASA 2-111 and they were powered by Rolls-Royce Merlins when the supply of Jumo 211 engines ceased.

Left: The **Firefly** remained in FAA service throughout the Korean War, where it served as a ground-attack aircraft. Firefly AS.5 WB271 was operated by the RN Historic Flight and is seen landing at Liverpool-Speke in June 1981. Sadly this aircraft was written-off in a fatal crash at Duxford.

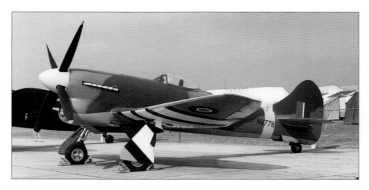

Above: Developed from the Typhoon, the **Hawker Tempest** was a single-seat fighter-bomber powered by a Napier Sabre engine of 2,180hp. Tempest TT.5 NV778/8386M is pictured at RAF Abingdon in June 1968. It is now an exhibit in the RAF Museum at Hendon.

Below: The **Tempest II** was the RAF's last piston-engined fighter to enter service. The powerplant for the variant was the 2,526hp Bristol Centaurus. N607LA/LA607 is pictured at Lakeland in April 2005; it is now part of the Fantasy of Flight collection at Polk City, Florida.

Avro's Lancaster bomber was the most famous of all the heavies used in World War Two. Still to be found in service with the Battle of Britain Memorial Flight is **Lancaster B.1** PA474. It is pictured landing at RAF Fairford in July 1997.

Above: An ex-French Navy **Lancaster**, G-ASXX/NX611, flew back to the UK in the 1960s. It moved to different locations and had a number of owners, during which time it ceased to be airworthy. It is pictured, in June 1989, at its base of East Kirby with the Lincolnshire Aviation Heritage where it performs engine-runs and can taxi around this ex-bomber airfield.

Left: Canada has the only other **Lancaster** still flying, which is part of the Canadian Warplane Heritage collection. C-GVRA/KB726 is pictured at its Hamilton, Ontario base in September 2005.

Canada's preserved **Lancasters** include FM159, with the Nanton Lancaster Society Museum in Alberta. It is in the markings of the aircraft flown by Squadron Leader Ian Bazalgette VC DFC – the only Albertan awarded the Victoria Cross.

Lancaster 10 FM136 is pictured as part of the Aero Space Museum of Calgary, in August 2005. It is currently under restoration, as can be seen the front turret is still to be fitted.

Above left: With its twin-boom shape the **Lockheed P-38 Lightning** was one of America's most distinctive fighters. P-38F NX17630/41-17630 has had a remarkable history. In July 1942 it was part of a flight of six forced down in Greenland and abandoned to sink into the ice. It was recovered in the early 1990s and restored to flying condition. It is pictured flying at Lakeland, Florida in April 2005; it carries the apt name *Glacier Girl*.

Above right: This **P-38L Lightning**, N25Y, is one of the original aircraft in the fleet of the Confederate Air Force. It is seen displaying at Reno, Nevada in September 1988.

Left: A dedicated reconnaissance version of the **Lightning** was produced under the designation F-5. F-5G N90813/44-53247 is pictured at the Pima County Museum, Arizona in October 1984. It was later shipped to the Musée de l'Air in Paris and was destroyed in a hangar fire in 1990.

Above left: A three-crew light bomber, the **Fairey Battle** was obsolete by 1939 yet remained in service for another year. The type then found a second role in training air gunners in Canada. Battle 1T R7384 shows off a bright yellow training scheme together with a gun turret at Canada's national collection at Rockcliffe in September 2005.

Above right: A Finnish development of the Brewster Buffalo, the **Valtion Humu** was powered by a Russian M.63 radial engine of 1,100hp in place of the US-fitted Wright Cyclone of 850hp. HM-671 is on show at the Finnish Air Force Museum at Tikkakoski in June 1998.

Right: First flown in 1938, the **Dewoitine D.520** was a French single-seat fighter. The powerplant was a 910hp Hispano-Suiza liquid-cooled piston engine. Production continued after the fall of France in 1940, as they were used by the Vichy Air Force. No 277 is on display at the Musée de l'Air, Paris in May 1983.

Right: Russia's Yakovlev Yak-7 was intended as a two-seat conversion trainer for pilots going on to all types of single-seat fighters. It proved to have such a good performance that it was itself changed to a single-seater. Pictured flying at Lakeland, Florida in April 2005 is **Yak-7UTI** N7YK. This privately-owned aircraft has been converted from a post-war Yak-11.

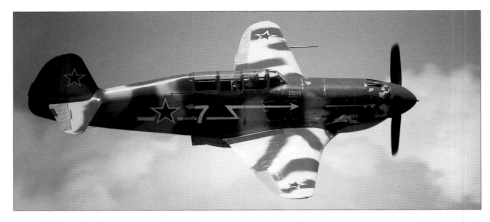

Below: Finland designed and built a fighter basically of wood. The **Pyorremyrsky PM1** was powered by a Daimler-Benz DB605 liquid-cooled engine. Two were ordered by the Finnish Air Force in 1942, with just a single example built. It was flight-tested between 1945 and 1947 and found to be an excellent machine for its role. PM-1 is displayed at the Finnish Air Force Museum at Tikkakoski in June 1998.

Fokker in Holland produced the **D.XXI** fighter in 1936. It was powered by a Bristol Mercury radial of 830hp. Finland both bought the type and licence-produced it. As an alternative to the British engine the Finns fitted an American Twin Wasp. FR-110 is at the Finnish Air Force Museum in June 1998.

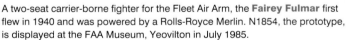

A two-seat carrier-borne fighter for the Fleet Air Arm, the **Fairey Fulmar** first flew in 1940 and was powered by a Rolls-Royce Merlin. N1854, the prototype, is displayed at the FAA Museum, Yeovilton in July 1985.

In the early days of World War Two the backbone of bomber command was the **Vickers Wellington**. N2980 is shown undergoing restoration at Brooklands in April 1993. This aircraft was rescued in the 1980s from Loch Ness where it had crashed during a wartime mission.

Despite having made a valuable contribution to Bomber Command in the early years of World War Two, no examples of the **Handley Page Hampden** were preserved. This airframe, P5436, was restored following a World War Two ditching whilst on a training flight in Canada. It is now displayed at the Canadian Museum of Flight & Transport at Langley, British Columbia, where it was photographed in September 2005.

Boeing B-29 Superfortress 44-86292 *Enola Gay* flew into the history books when it dropped the first atom bomb over Hiroshima on 6th August 1945. The aircraft, pictured at Silver Hill in May 1989, is now part of the NASM collection at Washington-Dulles Airport

Above: As the finest American bomber of World War Two, the **B-29 Superfortress** bore the brunt of the air attacks on the Japanese mainland. The type later served as an airborne tanker. N3299F/44-61669 is displayed, in October 1984, at March AFB, California, as *Mission Inn*.

Below: India was a source of **B-24 Liberator** airframes as they were used for maritime patrol into the 1970s. HE877/44-44175 is in Indian markings at Pima County Museum in October 1979.

The Texas-based Commemorative Air Force flies the only currently airworthy **Boeing B-29** on the American airshow circuit. N4249/44-62070 *Fifi* is seen performing at its then Harlingen base in October 1979.

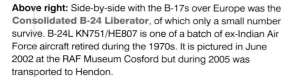

Above right: Side-by-side with the B-17s over Europe was the **Consolidated B-24 Liberator**, of which only a small number survive. B-24L KN751/HE807 is one of a batch of ex-Indian Air Force aircraft retired during the 1970s. It is pictured in June 2002 at the RAF Museum Cosford but during 2005 was transported to Hendon.

Right: One of the aims of the Commemorative Air Force is to keep its machines in the air and to tour. **LB-30 Liberator** N24927 is seen at Boscombe Down in June 1992, on a visit to the UK. This was the transport version of the type.

Below: The **Consolidated PB4Y Privateer** was a maritime patrol version of the B-24 with a single tall fin the main external difference. The type was still in service as a water-bomber protecting the forests of America until 2003. N3739G is pictured as an air-tanker with T&G Aviation at their Chandler, Arizona base in October 1984. It is now with the Lone Star State Flight Museum at Galveston, where it is being reconverted into military configuration.

Seen at the US Navy Museum at Pensacola, Florida, in April 1994, is a **PB4Y-2 Privateer**. It is a composite of N7682C/66261 together with parts of N2870G/66304 and was a water-bomber at one time.

A light bomber first flown in 1942, the **Douglas A-26/B-26** Invader has fought in three wars for the Americans; World War Two, Korea and Vietnam, as well as seeing action with other nations. A-26C FAC 2504/44-35508 is a gate guard at Gomez AFB, Colombia in September 1997.

Above: Many of the multi-engined warbirds flying today do so because they operated in the years after World War Two as water-bombers guarding the forests of the USA and Canada. One of the most prolific types used was the **Douglas A-26 Invader**. It was operated in Canada until as late as 2004. When such aircraft are retired from this role they are usually converted back to 'stock' in period military markings. It is therefore nice to see one museum keeping alive this important task by the retention of water-bomber colours. A-26 CF-BMS is in the livery of Canadian operator Conair at the West Coast Museum of Flying at Sydney, British Columbia, in August 2005.

Left: Before the days of the corporate jet, light bomber conversions provided executive transports. **Douglas A-26s** were converted by several companies including the On Mark Company's Marksman. N142ER/41-39215 has been re-converted back to military markings as a USN JD-1 '77141' and is at the Pensacola Museum in April 1994.

It is not common for the same aircraft to have different names and designations even within the same air force. Such a case was the Douglas DB-7 or A-20, Havoc or Boston. Its role was as a medium attack bomber, night fighter and intruder. Pictured in February 2003 at the RAAF Museum, Point Cook, Victoria is **DB-7 Boston III** A28-8.

One of the most widely-used light bombers of World War Two was the **North American B-25 Mitchell**. Its most famous single operation was the first bombing raid on Japan when US Army Air Force aircraft flew from the USS *Hornet* in April 1942. B-5-40/44-30369 is a Venezuelan Air Force example displayed at the air force museum at Maracay in November 1992.

Right: **B-25 Mitchells** served with many air forces, especially South American. Seen, in November 1992, displayed on a traffic island in the Bolivian city of Cochabamba is FAB 542.

With very distinctive nose art, **TB-25N Mitchell** N201L is on the ramp at Chino, California in September 1988.

Above: B-25 Mitchells are one of the most common light bombers to be found in museums in South America. B-25J 156/5087 was sold by the Brazilian Air Force to Uruguay. Following retirement it is pictured, in October 2003, at the Museo Aeronautico in Montevideo.

Right: The oldest **B-25 Mitchell** airframe is NL2825B/40-2168. This RB-25 is marked *Miss Hap* and was used during World War Two as the personal transport of General 'Hap' Arnold. It is seen at an airshow at Lakeland, Florida in April 1994.

Left: Canada used the **B-25 Mitchell** for pilot training in the post-war period. CF-NTU is marked as '1577' as it guards the gate of the CAF base at Winnipeg, Manitoba in June 1990.

Below: Perhaps the most versatile piston-engined warplane ever, the **de Havilland Mosquito** operated in a fighter/bomber/reconnaissance role as well as many others. It is a delight that the prototype of such an historic aircraft is preserved. W4050 is pictured in October 1986, the star exhibit at the Mosquito Aircraft Museum at Salisbury Hall near St Albans.

The **Martin B-26 Marauder** was a World War Two medium bomber with a production run of over 5,000 airframes; very few survive today. N4297J/40-1464 is pictured in April 2005 at the Fantasy of Flight Museum, Polk City, Florida.

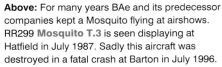

The only airworthy **Mosquito** is N35MK/RS712, a TT.35. It is seen at an airshow at Hamilton, Ontario in June 1990. It is currently on loan to the EAA Museum at Oshkosh, Wisconsin.

Above: For many years BAe and its predecessor companies kept a Mosquito flying at airshows. RR299 **Mosquito T.3** is seen displaying at Hatfield in July 1987. Sadly this aircraft was destroyed in a fatal crash at Barton in July 1996.

Right: Large parts of a **Mosquito FB.26** 6691 are pictured, in October 1999, at the China Aviation Museum at Datang Shan.

As late as 1963 the **Mosquito** was used by the RAF as a target-tug. It is from these that most of the current survivors come. TA639/7806M, another TT.35, is at the RAF Museum, Cosford in April 1991.

During the 1950s the Belgian Air Force operated **Mosquito NF.30** night fighters. They were ex-RAF machines. MB24/RK952 is pictured, in June 1983, at the Royal Army Museum, Brussels.

In terms of numbers, the **North American P-51 Mustang** is the most popular of all the warbird fighters. An ample supply of airframes and spare parts has ensured this. P-51A N51Z is one of the earliest still airworthy. It is seen at Oshkosh, Wisconsin in August 1986.

Seen in its hangar at Van Nuys, California, in October 1984, is **P-51C Mustang** N51PR; note the cockpit canopy of the early marks.

Left: The **P-51D Mustang** was the most widely-used variant and this is reflected in the numbers preserved. SE-BKG belongs to the Swedish Veteran Wing Museum at Västerås. It is seen visiting an airshow at Tampere in Finland in June 1998.

Below: After service with the Swedish Air Force this **P-51D Mustang** was supplied to the Dominican Air Force. When pictured in November 1992, FAD 1914 was a gate guard at air force headquarters in Santo Domingo.

A spectacular colour scheme is sported by **P-51D Mustang** N335/44-72902 at the Champlin Fighter Museum, Arizona in October 1998. It is one that the aircraft raced in.

Man o' War is the name of **P-51D Mustang** NL44727 as it flies over Oshkosh, Wisconsin in August 1986.

Above: The Mustang was built in Australia as the **Commonwealth CA-18**. VH-JUC/KH677 is pictured in February 2003 at its base of Tyabb, Victoria. It is part of the Old Aeroplane Company collection.

Right: **P-51D Mustang** NL38JC/45-11553 flies as *The Jacky C* in one of the more colourful of squadron markings. It is pictured at Lakeland, Florida in April 1984.

Above left: It is a refreshing change to see a **P-51D Mustang** in non-military markings. Canadian C-FFUZ is at Oshkosh in August 1986.

Above right: Final production version of the Mustang was the **P-51H**, which has a taller fin. 44-64265 is pictured, in July 1986, at Chanute AFB, Illinois.

Left: In the 1960s Cavalier Aircraft of Florida began complete re-builds of Mustangs for either the private market or as a low-cost COIN (counter-insurgency) aircraft. **Cavalier Mk.2** FAB 522/67-14865 is in Bolivian markings at the Venezuelan Air Force Museum, Maracay, in November 1992.

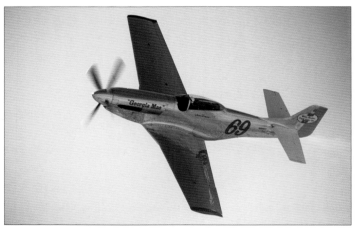

Above left: The **Mustang** is one of the most popular aircraft types used in Unlimited racing. NX10607 (No 69) is basically a stock aircraft and is pictured rounding the pylons at Reno, Nevada in September 1988.

Above right: Very much a racing special, **P-51 Mustang** N332 (No 84) is named *Stiletto*. The very low-drag cockpit is apparent as it taxies along the ramp at Reno in September 1988.

Right: A re-engined racing special, **P-51 Mustang** N5483V (No 09) is named *Precious Metal*. As well as the low-drag canopy it has contra-props on its Rolls-Royce Griffon, fitted for racing. It is pictured on the ramp at Reno in September 1988.

Right: Noted for having a wingspan nearly twice the length of the fuselage, the **Hurel-Dubois HD34** was a photographic-survey aircraft. It was used by the French IGN (Institut Géographique National) at Creil. F-BHOO is pictured at RAF Fairford in July 1987, attending an airshow from its base at Étampes.

Below: First flown in May 1963, the **Dassault Mystère 20** (Falcon) was the first of a long line of French biz-jets. The prototype F-WLKB is seen, in May 1983, in the Musée de l'Air, Paris.

Above: Very few airliners have been preserved in comparison with military types. However, this **Sud Aviation SE-210 Caravelle VI-R** N902MW is seen in July 1986 at the New England Air Museum, Connecticut. It is in the colours of Airborne Express, the parcel cargo carrier with which it last served.

Left: This **Sud Aviation SE-210 Caravelle**, No 141, was used by the French Air Force for VIP operations. Now retired, it is seen at the Musée de l'Air in May 1983.

Below left: Another VIP aircraft, albeit from an earlier era, is **Junkers Ju 52/3M** FAC 625, used by the President of Colombia. It is pictured in the air force museum in Bogotá in November 1992.

Above: The Swiss Air Force bought three of the famous German tri-motor transports in the 1930s and flew them until the 1980s. They were then operated by JU-Air for pleasure flights through the Alps. **Junkers Ju 52/3M** HB-HOP is seen with all three BMW engines running at its Dubendorf base in August 1987.

Left: Spain licence-produced the Ju 52 as the **CASA 352**. They were used as transports right into the 1960s. Many have been sold to warbird operators and museums, who usually paint them in German markings. G-BFHG/VK+AZ is at North Weald in May 1992.

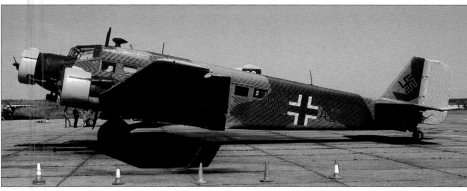

A biz-jet with swept-forward wings, the German-built **HFB 320 Hansa** first flew in 1964. It achieved limited success. D-CARE is owned by the Luftwaffe Museum. It is now on loan to the LSF Museum at Finow where it is pictured in May 2004.

Above: An interesting conversion of CASA 352 T2.B-148 produced a **Junkers Ju 52/1M**. The original aircraft was powered by a single 800hp engine. One of the five produced was sold in Canada. It is a replica of this aircraft, CF-ARM, that is on show at the Western Canada Aviation Museum in Winnipeg, Manitoba in June 1990.

Right: The **Nord 2501 Noratlas** was a medium tactical transport that served the French Air Force, which operated more than 200. F-AZVM is the last airworthy example and is based at Marseille-Marignane. It is pictured at an airshow at Coventry in August 2000.

As well as the large French use of the **N2501 Noratlas**, the Luftwaffe also operated the type, with aircraft being built in Germany. 99+14 is pictured at the Luftwaffe Museum at Gatow, Berlin in May 2004.

Above: There are few Chinese-designed and built aircraft. One is the **Harbin Y-11**, a light transport aircraft powered by a pair of radial piston engines. 352 is seen in use as a training aid at Tianjin in October 1999.

Left: First flown in 1947, the **Dassault MD.315 Flamant** was a light multi-purpose transport and communications aircraft. F-AZFX is preserved and flies at airshows. It is seen at Coventry in August 2000.

Specially designed as an agricultural spray aircraft, the **PZL M15 Belphegor** must be the only ag-plane powered by a jet engine, in this case a 3,300 lbst Ivchenko. CCCP-15105 is at the Monino Museum, Moscow in August 1995.

Designed and built by the Peking Aeronautical Institute, the **Peking/Beijing NR1** was a light feederliner powered by a pair of Russian radials. 0001 is seen displayed at the institute in December 1987.

A COIN (counter-insurgency) aircraft, the **FMA IA-58 Pucará** is Argentine-built and powered by a pair of Astazou turboprops. A533 is pictured at RAF Finningley in September 1982, following its capture during the Falklands War. The front fuselage is now on display with the Wiltshire Historic Aviation Group.

The first aircraft to fly over the North Pole was the **Fokker F.VIIa/3M**. It was flown by Floyd Bennett on Richard Byrd's 1926 expedition. BA1 is at the Henry Ford Museum at Dearborn, Michigan in July 1986.

Left: Still in service with the Russian Air Force as a bomber, the **Tupolev Tu-95** (*Bear*) is a swept-wing turboprop with high speed and long range. This early example (c/n 4807) is at the Monino Museum in August 1991.

Below: Russian manufacturer Beriev has a long history of producing flying-boats. First flown in 1949, the **Be-6** (*Madge*) was powered by piston engines. This Chinese example, 98706, has been re-engined with turboprops. It is at the China Aviation Museum at Datang Shan in October 1999.

With a production run of only one aircraft, the **CCF Burnelli CBY-3 Loadmaster** was not going to set the world alight. Its unusual shape comes from that the fact that it was designed as a lifting fuselage. It first flew in 1945, and performed trials with different powerplants. It last flew in 1959. N17N is seen at the New England Air Museum, Bradley Airport, Connecticut in July 1986.

Built with turboprops from the start is the **Beriev Be-12** (*Mail*). It first flew in 1960, and is still in service with the Russian Navy. '25 yellow' is at the Monino Museum in August 1995.

The **Yun-5** is a Chinese-built version of the 'go-anywhere, carry-anything' Antonov An-2. B-8452 is preserved as a training airframe at Tianjin in October 1999.

Beriev produced the **Be-30** (*Cuff*) for an Aeroflot requirement to replace the Antonov An-2. It lost out to the LET L-410 and only a handful were built. CCCP-67209 is a Be-32 with uprated engines, and is pictured in August 1991 at the Monino Museum.

Flown for the first time in 1955, the **Antonov An-8** (*Camp*) was a twin-turboprop tactical transport aircraft. A handful can still be found as tramp-cargo craft flying under registrations of convenience. '10 blue' is at the Monino Museum in August 1991.

A four-engined passenger airliner, the **Antonov An-10** (*Cat*) was developed from the An-8. First flown in 1957, it was withdrawn in 1973. CCCP-11213 is at the Monino Museum in August 1991.

A logical development from the An-10 was to add a rear door and produce a cargo version. This was designated the **An-12** (*Cub*). The aircraft can be found in service in many parts of the world today. B-3152 is an ex-Air China example used as a maintenance trainer at Tianjin in October 1999.

The Monino Museum near Moscow has examples of most Russian post-war designs. **Antonov An-12**, '04 blue', is pictured in August 1995 in Soviet Air Force markings.

Above left: A STOL light transport was next from the Antonov bureau. This was the **An-14** (*Clod*), locally named Pchyelka (Little Bee). 996 is in the markings of the old DDR air force, in May 2004, at the Flugplatzmuseum Cottbus.

Above right: The largest turboprop transport in the world, by a large margin, is the **Antonov An-22** (*Cock*). First flown in 1965, it is still in limited service with the Russian Air Force. CCCP-09334 is the largest Antonov at the Monino Museum in August 1995.

Left: In the late 1950s many companies, both East and West, were designing a range of DC-3 replacements. From Antonov came the **An-24** (*Coke*), the first in a line ending with the An-32. B-3414 is in the markings of CAAC and pictured, in October 1999, at the Guangzhou Technical Institute, China where it serves as a training aid to engineering students.

Above left: The An-24 was produced in China under licence as the **Xian Y-7**. B-3453 is in the livery of China Eastern Airlines in October 1999, and is a maintenance-training airframe at Tianjin.

Above right: First flown in 1945, the **Ilyushin IL-12** (*Coach*) was the first Soviet attempt at a 'modern' airliner, although to a far lower standard than equivalent western aircraft. China was one of the nations that received and operated the IL-12. 503 is in a poor state at the Tianjin technical training site in October 1999.

Right: It is not an unusual fate for an airliner to be converted into a restaurant. This usually occurs to an unwanted airframe that has sat for many years at the local airfield. It was quite different for **Ilyushin IL-14** RA-01146 as it was flown from Russia to Zurich, Switzerland in June 2005 to be used as the basis for 'Restaurant Runway 34'. The aircraft is pictured, prior to the move, at Moscow-Myatchkovo in August 1995.

Above left: All of Moscow's four passenger airports have gate guardians. **Ilyushin IL-14** CCCP-91484 is in the livery of Aeroflot at Bykovo in August 1995.

Above right: The **Ilyushin IL-14** (*Crate*) was an upgrade on the design of the IL-12. The most visible external difference was the square tail fin. It was also built under licence in Germany. DM-SAF is pictured, in May 2004, in the livery of Deutsche Lufthansa at the Junkers Museum, Dassau.

Right: Russia's first turboprop airliner, the **Ilyushin IL-18** (*Coot*), first flew in July 1957. It can still be found in service with third-world airlines to this day. IL-18D DDR-STE is pictured, in May 2004, in the livery of the now defunct East-German carrier Interflug at Borkheide, Germany.

Above left: Once the VIP transport for Chinese Prime Minister Chou En-lai, **Ilyushin IL-18** B-210 is pictured, in October 1999, as a training airframe at Tianjin.

Above right: Russia's first long-range jet airliner, the **Ilyushin IL-62** (*Classic*), first took to the air in 1961 and is still in service today. CAAC example B-2024 is at the China Aviation Museum at Datang Shan in October 1999.

Right: This early production **Ilyushin IL-62**, CCCP-86670, is in Aeroflot markings at the Monino Museum in August 1991.

The first wide-body airliner in Russia was the **Ilyushin IL-86** (*Camber*). First flown in 1976, it entered service four years later and is still operated by Aeroflot as well as a number of other airlines in former Soviet-bloc nations or republics. CCCP-86003 is the second production aircraft and is seen, in September 1995, with the Aeroflot Technical School at Sheremetyevo as an instructional airframe.

A licence-built version of the Douglas DC-3, the **Lisunov Li-2** (*Cab*) had a production run of nearly 5,000 airframes. 305, in CAAC markings, is a training aircraft at Tianjin in October 1999.

Antonov in Russia has produced a family of twin-engined turboprops starting with the passenger An-24. The military cargo version of this was the **An-26** (*Curl*); this had no cabin windows and featured a rear-loading ramp. One of the many air forces using the type was that of the DDR. When the 'two Germanies' re-unified the Luftwaffe inherited these aircraft. They were operated for several years before being disposed of. An-26SM 52+09 is pictured at the Luftwaffe Museum at Gatow, Berlin in May 2004.

Above: Entering service in 1940, the **Lisunov Li-2** served throughout the Great Patriotic War. This example is displayed, in August 1991, at the Army & Military Museum in Kiev.

Below: Very few Russian historic aircraft can be found flying, so it was good to see **Lisunov Li-2** FLA-01300 filling a gap. It is pictured, in August 1995, at an airshow at Zhukovsky near Moscow. Note the door on most Li-2s is on the right-hand side. Sadly this aircraft was destroyed in a subsequent fatal crash.

Above: A small three-engined airliner with approximately 30 seats, the **Yakovlev Yak-40** (*Codling*) can be found in large numbers operating air services between the towns and cities of Russia and other nations. CCCP-87490 is seen as part of the Monino Museum collection in August 1991.

Right: With the same layout as its little brother, the **Yakovlev Yak-42** (*Clobber*) is a medium-range 120-seat airliner. Early production aircraft CCCP-42304 is pictured, in August 1995, at the Park of Economic Achievements in Moscow.

Above left: Few airliners have been derived from bombers. The **Tupolev Tu-114** (*Cleat*) was a development from the Tu-95 (*Bear*). The prototype, CCCP-L5611, is preserved at Monino in August 1991.

Above right: Now out of service, the **Tu-114** boasted many speed, height and range records. CCCP-76464 is seen, in August 1995, preserved at the gate of Moscow's Domodedovo Airport.

Left: Another bomber/airliner development was Russia's first jet passenger aircraft, the **Tupolev Tu-104** (*Camel*). This was created by fitting a new fuselage to the Tu-16 bomber. CCCP-L5412 is displayed at the gate of Vnukovo Airport, Moscow in August 1995.

Right: A scaled-down Tu-104, the **Tupolev Tu-124** (*Cookpot*) was developed for short-haul routes. CCCP-45025 is pictured at Monino in August 1991.

Below left: The **Tupolev Tu-134** (*Crusty*) first flew in 1963 and was powered by a pair of rear-mounted Soloviev D-30 turbofans. They can still be found in service in large numbers throughout the world. DDR-SCZ is pictured, in May 2004, at the Luftfahrt Museum Merseburg. It is in the livery of the old DDR airline Interflug.

Below right: First flown in 1968, the **Tupolev Tu-154** (*Careless*) has the same layout and size as the Boeing 727. It can be found in large numbers with many Russian airlines. CCCP-85005 is an early production machine pictured, in August 1995, in the Park of Economic Achievements in Moscow.

Russia's short-lived supersonic airliner programme featured the **Tupolev Tu-144** (*Charger*) which first flew at the end of 1968 and operated cargo services from Moscow to Alma-Ata at the end of 1976. Passenger operations did not start until 1977 and only lasted until May 1978. CCCP-77106 is a star exhibit at the Monino Museum in August 1995.

Above: When a number of Boeing B-29 bombers landed in Siberia following a bombing raid on Japan in 1944 they were kept by the Soviets who began a process of reverse-engineering. From this emerged the **Tupolev Tu-4** (*Bull*). '01 red' is part of the bomber collection at Monino in August 1995.

Left: A number of **Tupolev Tu-4s** were passed on to the Chinese. They have taken the design even further as can be seen by 4134, a turboprop conversion that acts as drone carrier; note the device under the wing. It is at the China Aviation Museum in October 1999.

Right: The most amazing conversion from the **Tupolev Tu-4** is the illustrated Chinese example. 4114 has not only been re-engined with turboprops but features a rotodome radar for its role as an AWACS aircraft. It is in the China Aviation Museum in October 1999.

Below: In the late 1950s and early 1960s many aircraft manufacturers around the world were building so-called 'DC-3 replacements'. None realised that the venerable Douglas design would outlive them all. From Japan came the **NAMC YS-11**. Like most of its kind it was powered by a pair of Rolls-Royce Dart turboprops. First flown in August 1962 it had a production run of nearly 200 and can be found in limited service to this day. The prototype, JA8611, is pictured, in October 2004, at the Museum of Aeronautical Sciences at Narita Airport, Tokyo.

A short-field, light-transport tri-motor, the **Northrop C-125 Raider** was in service with the USAF for only five years from 1950. YC-125A XB-GEY/48-0636 is at the Pima County Museum, Arizona in September 1988.

One of America's first-generation jet airliners, the **Convair 990** was the least successful in sales terms with just 37 aircraft being built. It was however the fastest airline until the advent of the SSTs. Following a career with NASA, Convair 990 N810NA is now preserved as a gate guardian at Mojave Airport, California. It is pictured in October 2001.

A heavy strategic turboprop freight aircraft, the **Douglas C-133 Cargomaster** first flew in 1956. It was designed to be able to carry ICBMs such as the Thor loaded through large rear freight doors. The fleet were withdrawn from service in the early 1970s. 56-2009 is pictured, in August 1986, at Chanute AFB, Illinois.

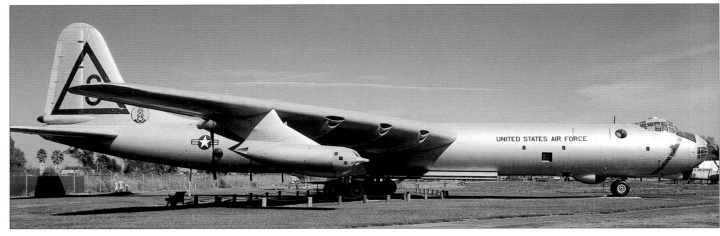

Above: Everything about the **Convair B-36** bomber was big. It could carry a bomb-load of 72,000 lb as normal, had a maximum range of 8,000 miles, and it had ten engines. There were six propellers as pushers together with four jets. RB-36H 51-13730 is on show at the Castle AFB Museum, California in October 2001.

Below: A battlefield surveillance aircraft, the **Grumman OV-1 Mohawk** has operated with the US Army in many roles since it entered service in 1961. 62-5860 is at the US Army Museum at Fort Rucker, Alabama in April 1994.

Part of a long line of rugged STOL transport aircraft, the **de Havilland Canada DHC-5 Buffalo** can be found in the air forces of many nations. Few have been preserved as yet. 322 of the Peruvian Air Force is in their museum at Las Palmas, Lima in September 1997.

Pictured in August 1987, this **Douglas DC-8-32** TU-TCP (c/n 45568) is an ex-Air Afrique example, now used by the airport authority at Zurich, Switzerland for various types of non-destructive training.

Beech Aircraft of Kansas has been producing a line of twin executive and utility aircraft for many years. **A65 Queen Air** 03-3095 is a retired Japanese example, and is pictured at the gate of Naha air base, Okinawa in October 2004.

Left: One of the first purpose-built biz-jets, the **McDonnell 220** was designed for the USAF UCX (Utility Transport Experimental) competition, which was won by the Lockheed JetStar. The sole aircraft built, N220N, is pictured in October 1984 at Albuquerque, New Mexico.

Below left: The first purpose-built COIN (counter-insurgency) aircraft was the **Rockwell OV-10 Bronco**. A two-seat turboprop twin, it first flew in 1965. The type has served with both the USAF and, as illustrated, the US Marine Corps as well as other nations. 155499 is at the Pima County Museum, Arizona in October 1998.

Below right: First flown in March 1949, the **Avro Shackleton** had a long service life in the RAF – first in a maritime patrol role and then as a radar-equipped early-warning aircraft. This second career lasted until the middle of 1991. Power was supplied by four 2,450hp Rolls-Royce Griffon liquid-cooled piston engines with contra-rotating propellers. Pictured in May 2003 is Shackleton AEW.2 WR963, it is a static exhibit owned by Air Atlantique as part of their historic collection at Coventry.

Above left: Learjets are one of the most popular of all the biz-jets in service today. Preserved examples are rare. **Learjet 25** N6NF is on show, in April 1994, outside a technical college at Ozark, Alabama.

Above right: This aircraft is an example of how the latest type can end up in a museum. The **Learfan 2100** was a small executive transport powered by a pusher propeller and largely made of carbon fibre materials. Production was planned in a factory in Northern Ireland but never went ahead. The sole aircraft, N626BL, is seen in May 2000 at the Museum of Flight at Boeing Field.

Right: Designed for non-stop transatlantic operations, only three examples of the **Sikorsky VS-44A** flying-boat were produced. The sole survivor, N41881, was used for services between Long Beach and Catalina Island until the 1960s. It is pictured at the US Navy Museum at Pensacola in October 1981, and is now on display at the New England Air Museum in Connecticut.

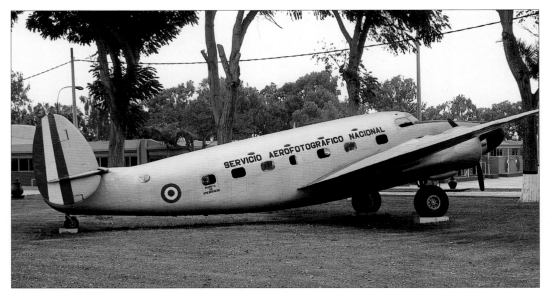

Left: A troop and freight transport aircraft, the **Lockheed C-60 Lodestar** was one of a range of developments from the manufacturer. Pictured in October 2003 at the gate of the NCO training school at Las Palmas, Lima is 512, formerly operated by the Servicio Aerofotographico Nacional of Peru.

Below: Winner of the USAF UCX competition, the **Lockheed JetStar** first flew as a twin-engined machine powered by a pair of Bristol Orpheus engines. N329J, the prototype, is pictured in September 1984 in a technical college in Vancouver, British Columbia.

Another of the Lockheed family of twins was the US Navy patrol bomber, the **PV2 Harpoon**. N7250C/84061 was a restored warbird and is pictured at Reno, Nevada in September 1988. It was destroyed in a fatal accident in California during 1990.

Production **JetStars** were equipped with four engines, these being P&W JT12s. The service roles of the type were as a VIP transport or flight calibration aircraft. VC-140B 61-2489 is in VIP markings at the Pima County Museum, Arizona.

Above: Used by the US military as a VIP transport or pilot/radar operator trainer, the **North American T-39 Sabreliner** was one of the first small biz-jet types to fly, in 1958. 62-4452 is on display at Travis AFB Museum, California in September 1988.

Right: A direct development from the B-29, the **Boeing B-50** was the same length and span. The engines, however, were much more powerful, being 3,500hp P&W R-4360s as opposed to the 2,200hp Wrights in the B-29. 49-310 is at the USAF Museum, Ohio in July 1986.

The Fairchild company in America licence-built Fokker Friendships. Two versions were manufactured, one a basic F-27 and the other the FH-227 that was stretched by 6ft 6in (1.98m). Pictured in October 2003 is Uruguayan Air Force **FH-227D** 572. It is now a gate guardian at their transport base at Montevideo Airport.

Based on a Stinson design, the **Faucett F-19** was first produced in Peru in 1934. It was a utility transport and could seat up to eight people. OA-BBQ is pictured on show at Lima Airport in October 2003.

Derived from the earlier 2-0-2, the **Martin 4-0-4** was a post-war airliner of similar configuration to the Convair 240. N636X is pictured at Oxnard, California, in October 2001. Operated by Airlines of America it is in the period livery of Pacific Air Lines and is available for charter work.

Developed from the L-188 Electra, the **Lockheed P-3 Orion** is one of the most successful maritime patrol aircraft in the world today. Pictured, in October 2003, at the Chilean Navy base of Vina del Mar is P-3A 401. This is one of a number of gate guardians and the interior has been converted into a museum of pictures and artefacts on the history of the base and air arm.

One of the first all-metal monoplane airliners, the **Boeing 247** first flew in 1933. N18E is part of the Science Museum collection and is pictured at Wroughton in September 1983.

Following the success of the Beaver, de Havilland Canada produced the **DHC-3 Otter**, a scaled-up aircraft powered by a single 600hp P&W R-1340. First flown at the end of 1951, it is still in widespread use in Canada where some have been re-engined with turboprops. NU-1B Otter 144572 is displayed, in April 1994, at the US Navy Museum at Pensacola.

Built as a flying-boat in 1939, the **Martin PBM Mariner** served the US Navy for many years as a patrol aircraft. The final version, an amphibian designated PBM-5A, closed the line ten years after the first flight. 122071 is at the Pima County Museum, Arizona, in September 1988.

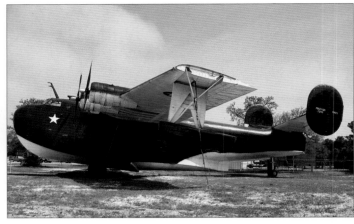

Based on the DC-2, the **Douglas B-18 Bolo** was a pre-war medium bomber. It had a brief front-line role but, after the Japanese attack on Pearl Harbor, it served on second-line duties only. 37-029/N52056 is at the Castle AFB Museum in California in October 1984. This airframe is a former water-bomber.

Above: A four-engined patrol-bomber flying-boat, the **Consolidated PB2Y Coronado** entered service with the US Navy in 1940. Front-line operations ended in 1945. 7099 is pictured at the USN Museum at Pensacola, Florida in April 1994.

Left: The **Grumman G-21 Goose** was the first in a line of amphibian flying-boats that served both in civil and military roles. N789 is pictured, in May 2000, at the Alaska Aviation Heritage Museum in Anchorage.

One of the most modern airliners of its day, the **Boeing 307 Stratoliner** had four engines and a pressurised cabin, and first flew in 1938. The last complete example, N19903, is pictured at the Pima Country Museum, Arizona in September 1988. Following its restoration by Boeing it is now at the new NASM museum at Dulles Airport, Washington DC.

Purchased off-the-shelf by the US military as the U-3, the **Cessna 310** was a twin-engined cabin monoplane for the private and business flyer. 57-5849 is a USAF example at the Castle AFB Museum, California, pictured in October 1984.

One of the few aircraft that can genuinely be said to have revolutionised flying is the **Boeing 747**. The prototype, N7470, is pictured in May 2000 at the Museum of Flight, Boeing Field.

A V/STOL transport aircraft with tilting wings, the **XC-142A** was produced by three companies, LTV, Ryan and Hiller, for a tri-service program. Its last use was with NASA at Langley. NASA 522 is pictured, in July 1986, at the USAF Museum in Dayton, Ohio.

A twin-boom, twin-engined troop and freight transport, the **Fairchild C-119** had a service life stretching from Korea to Vietnam, where it served as a gunship. C-119C 51-2566 is pictured, in April 1994, at Warner Robins AFB, Georgia.

During the 1960s some surplus **Fairchild C-119s** were converted to water-bombers to protect the forests of America. N13743 is one such airframe, and is pictured in the water-bomber park at the Pima County Museum, Arizona in October 1998.

Left: The last design from one of the world's oldest aircraft manufacturers was the Jetstream from Handley Page. It was an 18/20-seat pressurised turboprop-powered commuter aircraft. During the early production stages the company called in the Official Receiver and ceased trading. **HP.137 Jetstream 200** G-BBYM is pictured in June 2002 at the RAF Museum, Cosford. The design was taken up by British Aerospace and nearly 400 aircraft were subsequently produced.

Right: First produced as a five-seat light transport in 1939, the **Cessna T-50 Bobcat** was adapted by the USAAF as a pilot-trainer for crews going on to multi-engined craft. In civil markings, privately-owned Bobcat N99N is seen visiting Lakeland, Florida in April 1994.

Below: In 1969 the Brazilian government formed Embraer (Empresa Brasileira de Aeronautica SA). Since then it has grown to be a major producer of commuter airliners. The first design was the **EMB-110 Bandeirante**. It was also sold to military users for a variety of tasks. Pictured, in October 2003, at the Chilean Navy base of Vina del Mar is EMB-110CN 107, now relegated to gate guard duties.

At the end of World War Two Convair launched the **CV-240** airliner. First flown in 1947, it has been a great success and a few examples can be found in service today. XT-610 is in the livery of Central Air Transport and is without engines at the China Aviation Museum in October 1999.

Above: The **Convair CV-240** was exported to many parts of the world. Preserved at Aeropuerto Silvio Pettirossi, Asuncion, Paraguay is ZP-CDO. It is pictured, in October 2003, in the livery of the now defunct carrier Lineas Aereas Paraguayas.

Below: The **Aero Commander** range of light transport aircraft has produced a long line of executive transports from the 1948 first flight through turboprops to jets. All three US services have operated the type as the U-4 and U-9. In USAF markings at Warner Robins AFB, Georgia, in April 1994, is U-4B '37948'.

Stretching the CV-240 produced the **Convair CV-340**. Military as well as civil use was widespread, including casualty transport for twenty stretcher cases with the designation MC-131. C-131D 54-2806 is pictured, in September 1988, at Travis AFB, California. It was a former transport 'hack' for the Nevada ANG and has their nickname of *The High Rollers* on the fin.

Above: The second of three aircraft to have the name Globemaster, the **Douglas C-124** was a heavy strategic transport with two decks. 49-0258 is pictured in July 1986 at the SAC Museum at Omaha, Nebraska.

Left: For many years it was the world's largest aircraft, with the record for the shortest flight. Built by Howard Hughes, the **Hughes H-4 Hercules** was conceived as a troop transport for the Pacific theatre. It made a single flight of just over one mile at an altitude of 33ft above Los Angeles Harbor in 1947. Nicknamed the *Spruce Goose* it was hidden from the public before being displayed in a purpose-built dome at Long Beach, California, where N37602 is pictured, in September 1988. It has since moved to McMinnville, Oregon.

In production since 1954, the **Lockheed C-130 Hercules** still rolls off the manufacturer's lines today, albeit a very much updated aircraft. It has set the standard for tactical transport aircraft and will be flying for many years to come. C-130A A97-214 is a retired Royal Australian Air Force aircraft pictured, in February 2003, at their Point Cook museum in Victoria.

The military version of the Boeing Stratocruiser was the **C-97 Stratofreighter**. Both were derived from the B-29. C-97G 52-0898 is an ex-transport aircraft pictured at Chanute AFB, Illinois in August 1986.

Above left: The main use of the **C-97** was as a flying tanker for the SAC bombers. The last variant had a pair of J47 jets added under the wings to obtain the speed required for refuelling fast jets. KC-97L TK.1-03/123.03 (ex-53-0189) is pictured, in September 2002 at the Museo del Aire, Cuatro Vientos, Madrid. This aircraft was one of three operated by the Spanish Air Force.

Above right: Boeing Stratocruisers were the basis for one of the most drastic of aircraft modifications. This was the **Aero Spacelines Guppy** bulk transport, originally produced for NASA to move large sections of spacecraft around the USA. 377SG Super Guppy N940NS is pictured, in October 1998, in NASA livery at the Pima County Museum, Arizona.

Left: A mixed-power bomber, the **North American AJ Savage** had two P&W radials of 2,400hp as well as a single Allison J33 turbojet of 4,600 lbst in the tail. It was operated by the US Navy from carrier decks. AJ2 130418 is pictured, in April 1994, at the US Navy Museum at Pensacola, Florida.

Above left: The **Martin SP-5 Marlin** was the last flying-boat in service with the US Navy, and operated until the mid-1960s. Its role was maritime patrol. 135533 is at the US Navy Museum at Pensacola, Florida in October 1981.

Above right: First flown in August 1956, still in service in vast numbers, and with no direct replacement yet selected, the **Boeing KC-135** tankers of the USAF will fly on for many more years. The fleet has been modernised over time including fitting newer fuel-efficient engines. Early KC-135A 55-3139 has been retired to the Castle AFB Museum, California where it was pictured in October 2001.

Right: One of the most significant prototypes to be found today is that of the Boeing 707 range of airliners and flying tankers. N70700, designated **Boeing 367-80**, is pictured in store at Davis Monthan AFB, Arizona in September 1988. It is now at the NASM museum at Dulles Airport Washington DC.

Left: A short to medium-range version of the 707, the **Boeing 720** had a shorter fuselage and wingspan. HK-749 is in the colours of the Colombian national carrier Avianca. It is seen on display in a park in the capital, Bogotá, in September 1997.

Below: Smallest of the Grumman line of amphibians, the **J4F-1 Widgeon** entered service with the US Coast Guard in 1941. Naval operations followed. V212 is in USCG markings at the US Navy Museum, Pensacola, Florida in April 1994.

Military use of the 707 range has been extensive and varied and will continue for many years. They range from flying tankers to AWACS radar aircraft. Designated C-135 for most airframes, 55-3129 is an **EC-135P** airborne command post photographed, in October 1998, at the Pima County Museum, Arizona.

The second of a trio of four-engined piston-powered airliners, the **Douglas DC-6** is still in service today. DC-6B FAE 44691/HC-AVH is seen in September 1997 in the Ecuadorian Air Force Museum at Quito.

Above: Developed from the successful Hawker Siddeley (Avro) 748, the Andover was the military freight variant. It had a rear-opening cargo door and a 'kneeling undercarriage' to bring the cargo ramp to floor level. Pictured, in June 2002, at the RAF Museum, Cosford is **Andover E.3A** XS639/9241M. This was a conversion used for the calibration of navigation equipment at airfields.

Right: When used by the US military as a transport aircraft, the DC-6 served as the **C-118**. 53-3240 is a USAF VC-118A pictured in October 1979 at Pima County, Arizona. This was a VIP-configured aircraft and was used by American presidents up to JFK.

Ford Tri-Motors were operated by the US Navy as transport aircraft with the designations JR or RR. 9206/NC7861 is in naval livery at Pensacola, Florida in October 1981.

Dating back to 1926, the Ford Tri-Motor was one of America's first successful commercial airliners. **Ford 4AT-B** NX4542 is pictured at the Henry Ford Museum, Dearborn, Michigan in July 1986. This aircraft was the first to fly over the South Pole in 1929 as part of Richard Byrd's expedition.

Kept airworthy by the EAA and used for pleasure flying is **Ford 4AT-E** NC8407. It is pictured in its natural element at the EAA fly-in at Lakeland, Florida in April 1994.

Used in large numbers by the navies of the United States and other nations, the **Grumman S-2 Tracker** family had three main roles. First was that of anti-submarine search and attack, flown off the decks of carriers. S-2G N12-153600 is pictured in February 2003 at the Royal Australian Navy Museum at Nowra, New South Wales.

Left: Known in Canada as the **CP-121 Tracker**, this aircraft has the low-visibility markings commonly used today. 12188 is pictured in May 2000 at the CAF base at Comox, British Columbia.

Below: Last use of the S-2 airframe was as a carrier-on-board delivery aircraft. This variant, the **C-1A Trader**, had a new fuselage that could accommodate up to nine passengers or cargo. N475AM/136781 is a privately-owned example pictured, in October 2001, at California City.

The second main use of the Tracker airframe was as an airborne early-warning aircraft operated by the US Navy from carriers. It had a large radome on the top of the fuselage to carry the radar, and was known in service as the **E-1B Tracer**. 147212 is seen preserved on the USS *Intrepid*, New York in May 1989.

Designed to replace the C-130, the **Boeing YC-14** was a STOL transport first flown in 1976. Power came from two GE CF6 jets of 51,000 lb thrust each. The type was in competition with the McDonnell Douglas YC-15. Both flew, but the C-130 was not replaced and continues in production. 72-1873 is pictured at the Pima County Museum, Arizona in October 1998.

Above: A business turboprop, the **Mitsubishi MU-2** first flew in September 1963 and over 800 were built in the next twenty years. The type was noted for its very high performance. Pictured in October 2004 at the Museum of Aeronautical Science at Tokyo's Narita Airport is MU-2 JA 8628.

Left: Last of the great propliners, the DC-7 first flew in 1953. It had a relatively short career at the top, being replaced by the early jets and turboprops. This **Douglas DC-7C** was used by the French Air Force for its national space program. It had a radar dish mounted on top of the fuselage, which was used to track the launch and re-entry of satellites. 45061 is pictured in May 1983 with the Musée de l'Air in Paris.

Right: The **Lockheed 12 Electra Junior** followed the Lockheed 10; it was smaller and its role was as a feederliner or for the business user. N93R is owned by a vintage aircraft company and is seen at Grass Valley, California in September 1988.

Below: First flown in March 1971, the **CASA 212 Aviocar** has proved to be a great success as a light STOL transport for air forces worldwide. Power comes from a pair of Garrett TPE 331 turboprops of 900shp. The first production aircraft, TR.12A-3, is pictured in September 2002 at Madrid's Museo del Aire.

Although the same configuration as the DC-3, the **Curtiss C-46 Commando** was a much larger and heavier aircraft. Its role was the same – troop and cargo transport. 42-101198 is marked *Georgia Peach* at the Warner Robins AFB Museum, Georgia in April 1994.

Right: Still flying with the then Confederate Air Force is **C-46 Commando** N53594 *China Doll*. It is operated by the Southern California Wing at Camarillo, where it was pictured in September 1988.

Below left: With the **DHC-6 Twin Otter**, de Havilland in Canada produced one of the most successful commuter aircraft ever built. The first flight was in May 1965 and the type is still in service in very large numbers. Retired and preserved aircraft are very rare. Pictured in August 2005 at the Aero Space Museum of Calgary is DHC-6-100 C-FPAT in the livery of Kenn Borek Air, a local Alberta-based carrier which operates a large fleet of the type. This airframe was the second Twin Otter built.

Below right: Developed from the B-18, the **Douglas B-23 Dragon** was the first American bomber to have a tail turret. It had a short front-line life, soon being relegated to transport and secondary duties. N747M/39-033 is configured as an executive aircraft and is pictured on a visit to Travis AFB, California in October 1979. It was once owned by Howard Hughes.

Above left: First of the four-engined Douglas airliners, the **DC-4 Skymaster** first flew in 1942. Because of the war all the early production was of the military C-54 version. C-54E 44-9063/N88887 is pictured in June 2001 at Frankfurt's Rhein-Main Air Force Base. It is part of a memorial to the Berlin Air Lift; many hundreds of missions having been flown from this base.

Above right: Although it served in the military, this Colombian Air Force **Skymaster** is a civil-build DC-4 purchased from Scandinavian and used by the president for VIP trips. FAC 690 is pictured in November 1992 at the air force museum in Bogotá.

Right: South African Airlines operated an historic flight to display its aviation heritage. **Douglas DC-4** ZS-BMH is seen flying at Fairford in July 1998, while on a tour of Europe.

Canada produced a variant of the DC-4 with added cabin pressurisation and the powerplants changed to Rolls-Royce Merlins. It was known as the **Canadair C-4 North Star**. 17515 is pictured in July 1986 at the National Aviation Museum at Rockcliffe, Ontario.

A major user of the **HU-16 Albatross** was the US Coast Guard. Privately-owned N7029F/7218 is in the service's very smart colour scheme at Lakeland, Florida in April 1994.

Produced by Fairchild, the **C-123 Provider** was a tactical transport with a short-field performance. Pictured at Kulis ANG base, Anchorage, in May 2000, is C-123J 56-4395. This version had wingtip-mounted J44 jets and served in the Arctic and Alaska.

Above: Last of the Grumman amphibians, the **HU-16 Albatross** was used by the USN, USAF, and USCG for rescue and patrol work. It was also exported to many air forces around the world. HU-16B BS-02 is pictured at the Museo Nacional de Aeronautica, Moron, Buenos Aires in October 2003.

Below: First flown in September 1953, the **I.A.35 Huanquero** was designed as a multi-purpose aircraft. Its roles included crew trainer, transport, gunnery and bomb-aimer training and air ambulance. Power came from a pair of 620hp I.A.R. 19A air-cooled radials. It was an early example of Argentina producing both the airframe and the powerplants. A-316 is displayed in October 2003 at the national collection at Moron, Buenos Aires.

Above: Despite a number of these airframes being procured by water-bomber companies, only one aircraft was converted to this role. Now retired **C-123K Provider** N3142D is at Pima County, Arizona in October 1998.

Left: One of the main industries of Canada is that of timber. The vast nation has tens of thousands of acres of forest. It is therefore natural that the first and only specifically designed water-bombing aircraft comes from that country. The **Canadair CL-215** first flew in October 1967 and performed its first water take-off the following year. The aircraft has been sold to government agencies and air forces worldwide, particularly in the Mediterranean countries where there is a high risk of summer fires. A turbine-powered version, the **CL-415**, has replaced some of the earlier piston-powered models. UD.13-1 was the first CL-215 in service with the Spanish Air Force and has been retired and put on display at the Museo del Aire, Madrid. It was pictured in September 2002.

CASA in Spain has built a number of indigenous transport aircraft. The largest type is the **CASA 207 Azor**. First flown in September 1955, it was powered by a pair of 2,040hp Bristol Hercules air-cooled radial engines. Production, including two prototypes, was just 22 airframes. T.7-6 is pictured, in September 2002, at the Museo del Aire, Madrid.

Above: As well as the 'J' model, the **C-123K Provider** also had jets to boost its performance. These were J85s of 2,850 lbst each and were under the wings. 555 is a Royal Thai Air Force example and is pictured, in November 1989, in its Bangkok museum.

Right: With the distinctive 'channel-wing' to give a better lift coefficient, the **Custer CCW-5** was first produced in 1964. It did not go into production. N5855V is pictured in May 1989 at the Mid-Atlantic Air Museum, Reading, Pennsylvania.

Left: From the late 1940s to the early 1960s, the **Lockheed P2V Neptune** was the US Navy's front-line maritime patrol aircraft. Pictured in October 1981 is XP2V-1 89082, named *Truculent Turtle*. This aeroplane, preserved at the USN Museum, Pensacola, established a world distance record for straight-line flight in 1946, when it flew from Perth in Western Australia to Port Columbus in Ohio: a distance of 11,235 miles in 55 hours, 17 minutes.

Below: The final production version of the **Neptune** was the P2V-7 (SP-2H). In addition to the two 3,500hp R-3350 radial piston engines, it had a J34 turbojet under each wing, producing 3,400 lb of static thrust. VH-IOY/A89-273 is pictured in February 2003 at Illawarra, New South Wales and is operated by Australia's Historic Aircraft Restoration Society.

Guarding the gate at Jacksonville NAS, Florida in April 1994 is **P2V-5 Neptune** 131410. This variant had the highest production run.

USAF use of the **Neptune** was in the ELINT (Electronic Intelligence) role with the designation RB-69A. Illustrated is an ex-USN P2V-7 147954 painted as USAF '44037'. It is at Warner Robins AFB, Georgia in April 1994.

Above: First in a line of Canadian STOL twins, the **de Havilland Canada DHC-4 Caribou** first flew in July 1958. Its ability to operate into remote and unprepared areas has made it a difficult aircraft to replace. Pictured, in September 2002, at Madrid's Museo del Aire is retired Spanish Air Force example T.9-25.

Left: Operated only by the RCAF, the **Canadair CL-28 Argus** was a maritime patrol aircraft and designated CP-107. It was based upon the Bristol Britannia but had Wright turbo-compound 3,700hp piston engines and no pressurisation. First flown in March 1957, it was in service until 1981. Pictured in September 2005 at the National Aviation Museum at Rockcliffe is CP-107 10742.

Right: In northern Canada and Alaska the **Beech 18** can often be found on floats working off lakes. N1047B is ex-Alaskan Coastal Airways, and is pictured in May 2000 at the Alaska Aviation Heritage Museum, Anchorage.

Below: The **Beech 18** is a popular warbird as it has a military history but is also a practical means of transport. N5063N/HB275 is pictured flying in an airshow at Old Warden, Bedfordshire in July 1989.

With a re-designed nose section the Beech 18 became the **AT-11 Kansan**. Its role was to train bombardier and gunnery students. Pictured in October 2003 is 101 in the livery of the Uruguayan Air Force at the Museo Aeronautico, Montevideo.

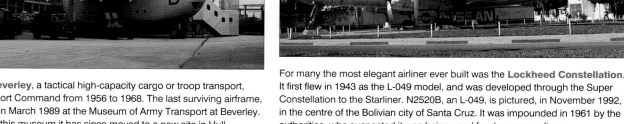

The **Blackburn Beverley**, a tactical high-capacity cargo or troop transport, served RAF Transport Command from 1956 to 1968. The last surviving airframe, XB259, is pictured in March 1989 at the Museum of Army Transport at Beverley. With the closure of this museum it has since moved to a new site in Hull.

For many the most elegant airliner ever built was the **Lockheed Constellation**. It first flew in 1943 as the L-049 model, and was developed through the Super Constellation to the Starliner. N2520B, an L-049, is pictured, in November 1992, in the centre of the Bolivian city of Santa Cruz. It was impounded in 1961 by the authorities, who suspected it was being used for drug-smuggling.

A star of the airshow circuit was **L-749 Constellation** N494TW/48-0609. It flew in the markings of MATS (Military Air Transport Service) and is seen at Fairford, in July 1998, during a European tour. In April 2005 the aircraft was flown to a new home on the Korean island of Jeju. It has been painted in period markings of Air Korea and is now on static display at the Korean Air training school.

Above: The next production variant of the **Constellation** was the L-749, a long-range version. N9463/48-610 is pictured in October 1998 at Scottsdale, Arizona, awaiting sale. This aircraft served with the USAF as a VIP transport for President Eisenhower with the name *Columbine II*.

Below: The **L-1049 Super Constellation** had a stretched fuselage to give extra seating capacity. N6937C is operated by the 'Save-a-Connie' group at Kansas City. Their markings are in the style of period TWA livery. It is seen visiting Lakeland, Florida in April 1994.

Above: Trans World Airlines was the carrier most associated with the **Lockheed Constellation**. L-749 G-CONI/N7777G never actually flew with the airline but has been painted in its livery as part of the Science Museum collection at Wroughton, where it was pictured in September 1984.

Right: **L-1049F Super Constellation** N73544, following some years of operation at Camarillo in California, has moved to Europe with the Swiss-based Super Constellation Flyers Association under the sponsorship of watchmaker Breitling. It is pictured, in September 2004, in its natural element at Payerne, Switzerland.

Left: Australia has acquired a flying 'Connie' in the form of an ex-USAF **L-1049/C-121 Super Constellation**. Now registered VH-EAG, with its name on the roof and tip-tanks, it is operated by the Historic Aircraft Restoration Society. It is pictured in February 2003 at Avalon, Victoria.

Below: Final development of the Constellation range was the **L-1649 Starliner**. It had much longer wings and the longest range. N974R is at Polk City, Florida, in April 2005. It is owned by a private individual in Maine and is in the care of the Fantasy of Flight Museum.

Military use of the **Constellation** included employment as an airborne radar platform. EC-121K 141311 is a US Navy aircraft at Chanute AFB, Illinois in August 1986.

While still flying the type, the Royal Thai Air Force has put **C-47B** 2-8/90 (44-76517) in its Bangkok museum. It was pictured in November 1999.

Above: One of the most significant aircraft of all time, the **Douglas DC-3/C-47** has seen off most of the aircraft designed to replace it. The only true DC-3 replacement has been another DC-3! They are still to be found in service worldwide. ZA947 is operated by the RAF Battle of Britain Memorial Flight both as a transport aircraft and as a training aid for Lancaster pilots on tail-dragger operations. It is pictured at Fairford in July 1998.

Right: Pictured at the gate of Kulis ANG base, Anchorage, in May 2000, is **Douglas C-47A** N2273K/'0315497'. It carries the markings of a C-47 operated by the 144 ATS of the Alaskan ANG.

Above left: In 1956 the first aircraft landed at the South Pole. This was US Navy **Douglas R4D-5** 12418 named *Que Sera Sera*. It is pictured in October 1981 at the National Museum of Naval Aviation at Pensacola.

Above right: In Finland the DC-Association operates pleasure flights with **DC-3 Dakota** OH-LCH. It is finished in the livery of Finnish Airlines-Aero and is pictured at its Helsinki base in June 1998.

Left: The Hellenic CAA have preserved this colourful **Douglas C-47**, SX-ECF, outside their office at Athens-Hellenikon Airport. It is pictured in June 1993.

Right: Pictured at Fort Patria, Ecuador in September 1997 is **Douglas C-47** CA 47. It carries the title 'Escuela de Fuerzas Especiales' and obviously false engines and propellers. This location is the home of the army special forces.

Below left: Pictured, in February 2003, on display at Cairns Airport, Queensland is **Douglas DC-3** N5590C. It wears the markings VH-BPA and the livery of Bush Pilots Airways. This carrier, re-named Air Queensland in 1982, provided a lifeline for supplies and transport to the many outposts of this vast state.

Below right: Guarding the main gate at the air force HQ at La Paz, Bolivia, in November 1992, is **Douglas C-47** TAM 01.

Above: PLUNA (Primeras Lineas Uruguayas de Navigacion Aerea) is the current flag carrier for the South American nation of Uruguay. Like many airlines in that continent they have a long history, being formed in 1936. It is therefore fitting that the Museo Aeronautico in Montevideo has a **Douglas DC-3** formerly operated by them on display. CX-BDB is pictured in October 2003.

Below: In a very smart modern camouflage scheme is Colombian Air Force **Douglas C-47** FAC 1651. It is pictured, in September 1997, at the NCO Training School adjacent to Madrid AFB, near Bogotá.

Preserved at the Royal Netherlands Air Force Museum at Soesterberg, in June 1983, is **Douglas C-47** ZU-5. It had served with the Royal Danish Air Force and was sold to the Dutch for display.

Above: Forerunner of the DC-3 was the **Douglas DC-2**. Notice how the tail is a different shape. N39165/'PH-AJU' is in the markings of the aircraft that flew in the UK-to-Australia Air Race of 1934. It is photographed at Coventry in May 2003.

Left: The last Douglas-produced version of the DC-3 was the **C-117**. It featured more powerful engines and a revised tail together with other modifications. 50834 is pictured at the US Marine Corps Museum at Quantico, Virginia in May 1989.

Designed by Handley Page as a 'DC-3 replacement', the **HPR.7 Herald** was powered by a pair of Rolls-Royce Dart turboprops. No examples are left flying today. Seen in July 1991, preserved by the Duxford Aviation Society is G-APWJ, which wears the livery of Air UK.

A more successful 'DC-3 replacement' was the **Hawker Siddeley (Avro) 748**. Like the Herald, it was powered by a pair of Rolls-Royce Darts. FAE 682/HC-AUD is an Ecuadorian Air Force example retired to its museum at Quito after being damaged. Note the unusual shape of the repaired cockpit area. It is pictured in September 1997.

G-BSST, the first British-built **Concorde** to fly, is preserved in its own section of the Fleet Air Arm Museum at Yeovilton. This airframe was purely for test-flying and operated from 1969 until 1976, when it was retired. It is pictured in June 1977.

First flown in 1962, the **Vickers VC-10** entered service with BOAC two years later. It had four tail-mounted Rolls-Royce Conway jets giving a thrust of 21,000 lb each. G-ARVM is in the 1970s markings of British Airways, and is at the RAF Museum, Cosford in June 2002.

Designed for short and medium-haul routes the **BAC 1-11** has been a great success. Early sales were to some of the major American carriers. G-AVMO is in 1980s British Airways livery at the RAF Museum, Cosford in May 1993.

The **Avro Lincoln** was developed from the Lancaster, but was too late for World War Two service. It ended its RAF career on second-line duties as late as 1963. Thirty were exported to Argentina, both new-build aircraft and ex-RAF machines. Pictured at Moron in October 2003 is Lincoln B.2 B-004, marked as B-010. It was formerly RF351 in RAF service.

Above: A civil conversion of the Sunderland, the **Short S.25 Sandringham** operated passenger services until the mid-1970s. N814ML/ML814 is pictured at the Fantasy of Flight Museum at Polk City, Florida in April 2005.

Right: The French colonies in the South Pacific operated **Short Sandringham** services between the islands. F-OBIP is pictured, in May 1983, at the Musée de l'Air in Paris. It wears the livery of Tahiti-based airline Réseau Aérienne Interinsulaire.

Above left: Shorts developed the **S.45 Solent** from the Seaford flying-boat. It was powered by four Bristol Hercules 1,690hp radials. N9946F/ NJ203 is pictured at the Western Aerospace Museum at Oakland, California in October 2001.

Above right: A large-capacity bulk freighter, the **Armstrong-Whitworth Argosy** first flew in 1959 and entered service with RAF Transport Command in 1962. Powerplants were four Rolls-Royce Dart turboprops. XP411/8442M is pictured in May 1993 at the RAF Museum Cosford.

Left: Beside military use, the Argosy was sold to civilian operators. **Argosy 101** G-BEOZ is in the colours of Elan, a parcel-carrier, in July 1989 at the Aeropark at East Midlands Airport.

Right: In the 1950s and 1960s the **Bristol Freighter** could be found around the UK flying cars and their passengers to Ireland and the European mainland. Canada had the last operational aircraft. Mounted on a plinth at Yellowknife Airport, North West Territories in May 2000 is B.170 Mk 31 CF-TFX in the livery of Wardair.

Below left: The military of seven nations used the **B.170 Freighter**. Its nose doors made it easy to load bulky items. TC-330 of the Argentine Air Force is at the National Aeronautical Museum at Moron in October 2003.

Below right: An elegant airliner, the **Bristol Britannia** was one of a number of turboprops that had a short life with the major carriers before being replaced by pure jets. They did, however, go on to have a long and successful career with holiday charter operators. G-AOVF is pictured, in April 1991, wearing BOAC Markings at the RAF Museum, Cosford.

The last **Britannia** to fly was an ex-RAF example that had seen service as a cargo aircraft in Africa. EL-WXA has been preserved since 1997 by the Britannia Aircraft Preservation Trust at Kemble, where it is pictured in August 1999.

Designed for the needs of BEA, the **de Havilland DH.121 Trident** had only limited sales other than to its first customer. G-AWZU is pictured, in July 1994, as a non-destructive training aircraft used by the fire service at Stansted.

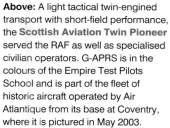

The last commercial use of the **Trident** was in China, where both CAAC and the air force used it. B-2219 is pictured in the livery of the former at the technical training school at Guangzhou in October 1999.

Above: A light tactical twin-engined transport with short-field performance, the **Scottish Aviation Twin Pioneer** served the RAF as well as specialised civilian operators. G-APRS is in the colours of the Empire Test Pilots School and is part of the fleet of historic aircraft operated by Air Atlantique from its base at Coventry, where it is pictured in May 2003.

Right: A large-volume, long-range strategic freighter built for the RAF, the **Short Belfast** had a brief service career before defence cuts ended it. One still flies for HeavyLift in Australia. XR371 is pictured, in May 1993, at the RAF Museum, Cosford.

First flown in 1946, the **Handley Page Hastings** was a workhorse for RAF Transport Command. Powered by four Bristol Hercules radials of 1,675hp, it was replaced at the end of the 1960s in the transport role by the C-130. TG528 is pictured at the Imperial War Museum at Duxford in July 1991.

One special version was the **Hastings T.5**. This was used by Bomber Command to train bomb-aimers. Under the fuselage it had a radome containing the radar bomb-sight equipment. TG517 is pictured, in August 1997, at the Newark Air Museum.

Above left: The **Vickers Viking** was Britain's first post-war transport aircraft. Parts used in its manufacture were the same as those in the Wellington bomber. T-9 is displayed in the livery of the Argentine Air Force at the National Aeronautical Museum, Moron, Buenos Aires in October 2003.

Above right: Developed from the Viking, the **Vickers Varsity** was a crew-trainer for the RAF. It could be used for pilot, navigator and bomb-aimer training on the same mission. WF369 is pictured in August 1997 at the Newark Air Museum.

Left: Entering service with the RAF in 1936, the **Avro Anson** served for more than thirty years. Its early years saw operations such as coastal patrols. N4877 Anson I is pictured at Staverton in May 1975. It is now part of the Imperial War Museum collection at Duxford.

Right: The last years of the Anson saw it in the communications role. Almost every RAF base had a station flight with an Anson on charge. **Anson C.21** G-VROE/WD413 is now operated by Air Atlantique as part of its historic fleet. It is pictured at its Coventry base in May 2003.

Below left: Ansons were built in Canada by Avro and used for pilot and crew training. **Anson V** C-FHOT/12417 is operated by the Canadian Warplane Heritage Museum at Hamilton, Ontario. It is pictured at this location in June 1990.

Below right: The world's first commercial jet operation began in May 1952 when BOAC services started between London and Johannesburg flying the Comet. **De Havilland DH.106 Comet 1XB** G-APAS/8351M is in period BOAC markings at the RAF Museum, Cosford in May 1989.

Final development of the series was the Comet 4C. N888WA is in BOAC markings at a technical training college at Everett, Washington, in August 1986. The aircraft never flew with this carrier but was painted in their period livery by Boeing.

When in 1937 it entered RAF service, the **Airspeed Oxford** was the first twin-engined monoplane advanced trainer to be adopted. It served throughout the war in the pilot-training role. V3388 is pictured at Staverton in May 1975, it is now in the care of the Imperial War Museum at Duxford.

First flown in 1948, the **Percival P.54 Prince** was a feederliner and executive transport. It also served the military in a communications role. BT1-1/96 is a Royal Thai Air Force example pictured, in November 1998, in its Bangkok museum.

Above: The most famous operator of the **de Havilland DHA-3 Drover** was Australia's Royal Flying Doctor Service. First flown in January 1948 the design was a simple, sturdy, eight-seat light transport powered by three 145hp Gipsy Major engines. VH-AND, a Drover Mk 2, is operated by Bathurst Vintage Joy Flights at Bathurst, New South Wales. It is pictured at base in February 2003.

Below: North America was a fertile sales ground for the **Viscount**. CF-THI is pictured in the markings of Trans Canada Airlines at the National Aviation Museum, Rockcliffe, Ontario in July 1986.

Above: One of the great successes of the British aviation industry is the **Vickers Viscount**. It first flew in 1948, and can still be found on cargo operations today, albeit in very small numbers. Viscount 701 G-AMOJ is in early BEA livery at the RAF Museum, Cosford in May 1989.

Right: The de Havilland DH.104 **Dove** was a light transport and executive aircraft powered by a pair of Gipsy Queen piston engines. The type sold in the hundreds worldwide. 2531 is pictured, in November 1992, in the Venezuelan Air Force Museum at Maracay.

First of a trio of de Havilland twins, the **DH.84 Dragon** flew in 1932. EI-ABI is operated as an historic aircraft by Aer Lingus from Dublin. It is seen at an airshow at Coventry in August 2000.

Two years after the Dragon came the **DH.89 Dragon Rapide**. It had a production run of more than 700. The family resemblance can be seen in its smoother lines. G-AIDL is pictured at its Coventry base in August 1999, where it is used for pleasure flights by Air Atlantique as part of their historic flight.

Last and most elegant of the three is the **DH.90 Dragonfly**. This first flew in 1935, but had a much shorter production run than the Rapide. G-AEDU is pictured at Cranfield in July 1982.

Above: The Boeing 727 was the world's best-selling airliner until it was overtaken by its baby brother, the 737. It racked up sales of 1,832 aircraft. The type can now mainly be found operating cargo services, with many of the early short-body series having been stored or scrapped for spare parts. **Boeing 727-22C** C-GBWA of Morningstar Air Express is pictured at Hamilton, Ontario, in September 2005. This Edmonton, Alberta-based carrier had leased the aircraft from small-parcel-delivery giant Federal Express and operated it on their behalf. It has now been retired and will be used by the Canadian Warplane Heritage as a classroom to teach schoolchildren their aviation history.

Left: The **Westland (Bristol) Belvedere** was the RAF's first twin-rotor, twin-engined helicopter. It had a short operational life, entering service in 1961 and retiring at the end of the decade. XG454/8366M is pictured in December 1987 at the Manchester Museum of Science & Industry.

Designed to operate on the Royal Navy's anti-submarine frigates, the **Westland Wasp** can be armed with torpedoes. XS570/A2699 is being used as a training airframe at RNAS Lee-on-Solent in July 1987.

Lockheed's AH-56 Cheyenne was a fast-attack helicopter. It suffered development problems and political pressure, which all resulted in the design being cancelled. 66-8832 is pictured at the US Army Museum at Fort Rucker, Alabama in April 1994.

Left: In an autogiro the blades are not driven by the engine but by forward velocity. The Spanish inventor Don Juan de la Cierva produced the first practical machines. **Cierva C.8L** G-EBYY used the fuselage of an Avro 504. The aircraft flew from London to Paris in 1928 and is pictured, in May 1983, in the Musée de l'Air, Paris.

Below: Two variants of the **Saunders-Roe Skeeter** were produced. One was an air-observation post for the Army and the other was a dual-control trainer for the RAF. XL813 is the former as an AOP.12 at the Army Air Corps Museum, Middle Wallop, July 1984.

The Boeing-Vertol 107 is a tandem-rotor, twin-engined, medium transport helicopter. It first flew in 1958 and is known in the Canadian Armed Forces as the **CH-113 Labrador**. It is currently being replaced by the new EH Industries Cormorant. The RCAF Museum at Trenton has received one for display. Pictured in September 2005, CH-113A 11315 awaits restoration to display standards.

Three examples of the **McCulloch YH-30** helicopter were acquired for evaluation by the US Army in 1952. It was a small observation machine with tandem rotors driven from a single engine. It was not ordered into production. 52-5837 is pictured in October 1981 at the US Army Museum at Fort Rucker.

Above: The **Bristol 171 Sycamore** was a four/five-seat general-purpose machine. It served with the RAF as both an air-sea rescue and transport helicopter. XJ918/8190M is an HR.14 pictured at the RAF Museum, Cosford in April 1991.

Right: Seen at the Henry Ford Museum at Dearborn, Michigan, in July 1986, is NC799W, a **Pitcairn PCA-2 Autogiro**. It carries the name of *The Detroit News*, which flew it in the 1930s.

Left: Igor Sikorsky produced the first working rotor-driven helicopter with the **VS-300**. This first flew, tethered, in 1939 and in free flight the following year. By 1941 it was able to stay aloft for 90 minutes, creating a world record. NX28996 is in the Henry Ford Museum in July 1986.

Below left: First used by the US Navy, the **Piasecki H-25 Retriever** was adopted by the US Army. A single-engined twin-rotor, it was used as a utility helicopter. 51-16616 is pictured in April 1994 at the US Army Museum, Fort Rucker.

Below right: The Royal Canadian Navy used the Retriever under the designation **HUP-3**. 51-16623 is at the National Aviation Museum at Rockcliffe, Ontario in July 1986.

Above left: A military version of the popular Bell JetRanger, the OH-58 Kiowa is used for observation and liaison work. Pictured at the RCAF Museum, Trenton in September 2005, **CH-136 Kiowa** 136204 is in a special commemorative livery.

Above right: A shipboard anti-submarine helicopter, the **Kaman SH-2 Seasprite** serves on US Navy frigates and destroyers. 150185 is with the Museum of Alaska Transportation and Industry at Wasilla in May 2000.

Right: Bell's **YAH-63** twin-engined attack helicopter was designed for a US Army specification. It was up against the YAH-64 from Hughes and lost the resulting fly-off. The second prototype, 73-22247, is pictured in October 1981 at the US Army Museum, Fort Rucker.

Another helicopter that failed as the result of a fly-off was the **Boeing Vertol YUH-61**. It was in competition with the Sikorsky H-60 for a massive order to replace the UH-1. Three prototypes were produced and the first, 73-21656, is pictured in October 1981 at the US Army Museum.

Sud Aviation (later Aérospatiale) produced one of the most successful helicopters in the world with the Alouette. First flown in March 1955, the Alouette III followed four years later. Over fifty nations operate the type. Pictured at the Republic of Singapore Air Force Museum at Paya Lebar, in February 2003, is **Alouette III** 200. It wears the old air force roundel.

Left: A joint US Army/Navy project in 1962 for a high-speed, highly-manoeuvrable research helicopter resulted in the **Lockheed XH-51A**. Two were produced and the first, 151262, is pictured at Fort Rucker in October 1981.

Below: Following a US Army evaluation of the prototype CH-37, it was ordered into production as the Mojave. The clamshell doors in the nose were used for loading vehicles. **CH-37B** 55-0644 is at the Fort Rucker museum in April 1994.

Above: The first helicopter to see RAF service was the **Sikorsky Hoverfly** in the early part of 1945. Its powerplant was a single 180hp Warner engine. KK995 is pictured at Abingdon, in June 1968, and is now part of the RAF Museum at Hendon.

Below: Developed from the Mi-6, the **Mil Mi-10** (*Harke*) was designed as a flying crane with large, high undercarriage legs so it could straddle its cargo. Even a bus could be carried underneath. The illustrated example is seen at the Monino Museum, Moscow, in August 1991.

When it first flew in 1957, the **Mil Mi-6** (*Hook*) was by far the largest helicopter in the world. Its role was heavy-lift in remote areas of the USSR such as Siberia. '29 red' is at the Central Air & Space Museum, Moscow, in August 1995.

The Mi-4 was produced in China under licence as the **Harbin Z5**. More than 500 airframes were produced from 1959. 7272 is at the China Aviation Museum in October 1999.

Above: Known to NATO as the *Hound*, the **Mil Mi-4** was one of the most successful of the piston-powered Russian helicopters. The illustrated example is in the Central Air & Space Museum, Moscow, in August 1995.

Right: By far the largest helicopter ever built was the **Mil V-12** (*Homer*). Only two examples were produced. Seen at Monino in August 1995 is the second prototype, CCCP-21142, which first flew in 1969 and appeared at the Paris Air Salon in 1971.

Below: Produced on Stalin's orders in 1951, the **Yakovlev Yak-24** (*Horse*) was, for its time, a large and powerful transport helicopter. Yak-24U '51' is seen at Monino in August 1995.

Above: First flown in 1962, the **Sikorsky CH-54 Tarhe** was a heavy-lift, twin-engined helicopter for the US Army. It could operate as a flying crane or by carrying a pod that the tall undercarriage would straddle. 70-18488, a world record-breaker for time-to-height, is pictured in May 2000, preserved by the Alaskan National Guard at Fort Richardson.

Left: Helicopters from the Kamov design bureau are noted for their use of co-axial rotors. Produced to meet a need for shipboard anti-submarine operations, the **Kamov Ka-25** (*Hormone*) has led to a whole family of multi-role machines. '17 black' is at the Monino Museum in August 1991.

Above left: Pictured in August 1995 outside the Kamov OKB site in Moscow is the prototype **Ka-26** (*Hoodlum*) CCCP-26002. This model was a utility machine whose roles have included agriculture and firefighting.

Above right: A heavy attack helicopter, the **Mil Mi-24** (*Hind*) could also carry up to eight troops. It has evolved a great deal since it first flew in 1970. '05' is an early Mi-24A and was seen in August 1995 at the Central Museum of the Armed Forces in Moscow.

Left: The evolution of the *Hind* can be seen in this **Mi-25E** 4493, an Iraqi Air Force example captured during the 1991 Gulf War. This designation was for a down-graded version for export, as can be seen, the nose section has been redesigned. It is pictured at the Fort Rucker museum in April 1994.

Right: Although it never flew, the prototype **Boeing-Vertol XCH-62** 73-22102 is on show at Fort Rucker in April 1994. This helicopter was designed to replace the H-54 but development was stopped in 1975.

Below left: A turbine-powered version of the Mi-1, the **Mil Mi-2** (*Hoplite*) was passed to PZL in Poland for its entire production and development. The pictured example is at the Monino Museum in August 1991.

Below right: Renowned as a producer of light aircraft, the Cessna company of Wichita, Kansas, produced a helicopter in 1954. A number were evaluated by the US Army but a production order was not forthcoming. **Cessna YH-41** 56-4244 is pictured, in October 1981, at the Fort Rucker museum.

With its distinctive intermeshing rotor system the **Kaman HH-43 Huskie** was produced for the USAF as a dedicated crash rescue and firefighting helicopter. 62-4532 is seen at the Travis AFB Museum, California in September 1988.

The first deliveries of the **Sikorsky HH-52 Seaguard** to the US Coast Guard took place in 1963. Its role was in search and rescue. 1429 is pictured in May 1989 on the deck of USS *Intrepid* in New York.

One of the most famous helicopters is the **Bell 47G**. It was the first volume machine for the US Army, with more than 2,000 being received, and was also widely exported. 401 of the Peruvian Navy is pictured as a gate guard at the service's base at Lima Airport in October 2003.

Early experience in Vietnam showed the US Army that it needed a dedicated attack helicopter to provide support for troop-carrying machines. After a fly-off competition a production contract went to the **Bell AH-1G Cobra**. 71-15090 is pictured at the entrance to the US Army Museum, Fort Rucker in April 1994.

Left: When the US Army wanted a new LOH (Light Observation Helicopter), twelve companies submitted bids. The eventual winner was the **Hughes OH-6 Cayuse**. It also sold in the civil market as the Hughes 369. Pictured in November 1992, outside the headquarters building of the Dominican Air Force in Santo Domingo is one of the six OH-6s it operated.

Below: The first variant of what was to become a successful line of helicopters was the **Sikorsky YR-5A**. First flown in 1943, it was powered by a single P&W R-985 piston engine of 450hp. IKL-4/96 is pictured, in November 1999, at the RTAF Museum, Bangkok.

The **Mil Mi-8** (*Hip*) started life as a turbine-engined development of the Mi-4. It has led to countless variants and roles with worldwide operators both civil and military. HS-1 is a Finnish example, seen in May 1998 at the Finnish Aviation Museum, Helsinki.

Left: The next version from the R-5 was the **Sikorsky S.51/H-5**. This first flew in 1946, having a four-seat cabin and a nosewheel undercarriage. N92808/48-555 is seen, in October 1984, displayed at the Rescue Heritage Collection at Kirtland AFB, New Mexico.

Below: A general-purpose and troop-carrying helicopter, the **Vertol H-21 Shawnee** entered US Army service in 1954. N70881 is a privately-owned example, seen at Oshkosh, Wisconsin in August 1986.

A civil variant of the H-21, the **Vertol 44** was used for airport-to-city-centre travel, mainly in New York. N74056 was the only one exported to Russia and is seen at the Monino Museum in August 1991.

Used by all American armed services and widely exported, the **Sikorsky S.58/H-34** was originally designed to a US Navy requirement for anti-submarine work. It was powered by a single Wright R-1820 piston engine of 1,525hp. Displaying the smart livery of the Chilean Navy is 51 (ex-150730). It is pictured, in October 2003, at the national museum in Santiago.

Above: The USAF's first tandem-rotor helicopter was the **Vertol H-21**. It was used by MATS for rescue duties in the Arctic. 53-4366 is in a high-visibility scheme at the Rescue Heritage Collection at Kirtland AFB in October 1984.

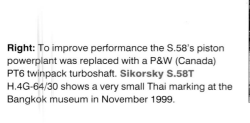

Right: To improve performance the S.58's piston powerplant was replaced with a P&W (Canada) PT6 twinpack turboshaft. **Sikorsky S.58T** H.4G-64/30 shows a very small Thai marking at the Bangkok museum in November 1999.

Left: Licensed production of the S.58 was undertaken in the UK by Westland, as the Wessex with a turbine engine. Both the RAF and Royal Navy used it for assorted roles. The civil variant was designated the **Wessex 60**. This had 16 passenger seats with a civil navigation and communications package. Several of these aircraft found military service later in their lives with the navy of Uruguay. 063 is now a gate guard at their base at Laguna del Sauce at Punta del Este. It is pictured in October 2003.

Below: All branches of the American armed forces use the UH-1. **UH-1F** 64-15495, a USAF example, is seen in October 1984, mounted on a plinth at Kirtland AFB.

With more than 9,000 bought by the US Army, it is no wonder that the **Bell UH-1 Iroquois** has become the face of army helicopter operations. 62-2018 is pictured, in April 1994, at the Alabama Welcome Centre on Route 231.

First flown in 1949 as the Sikorsky S.55, the **UH-19 Chickasaw** saw extensive US Army service from Korea to Vietnam. 51-14272 is seen with the engine access doors open at Fort Rucker in April 1994.

Above: Developed from the UH-1, the **Bell 212** is larger with capacity for 16 passengers. Power is supplied with a 1,290shp twinpack P&W PT6. Seen at the Peruvian Air Force Museum at Las Palmas, in September 1997, is 612.

Right: Before the army used the **Sikorsky H-19** the USAF introduced the type for rescue purposes and fitted a hoist on the starboard side. US Navy UH-19F 138499 is seen, in October 1984, at Kirtland AFB masquerading as H-19A 13893.

The Mil Mi-14 (*Haze*) was a development of the Mi-8 for naval operations. It featured a boat hull and the rear loading doors were deleted. The undercarriage retracted into external pods. Pictured at Peenemünde airfield, in May 2004, is **Mil Mi-14PL** 95+05, an ex-DDR aircraft used for a short time by the Luftwaffe.

Below left: Ordered into production in 1918, the **Junkers J9/D1** was a monoplane in the days of biplanes and all-metal in an era of fabric and wood. 5929 is pictured at the Musée de l'Air in June 1977, then based at Meudon but now at Le Bourget.

Below right: The Brandenburg W33 was a World War One German floatplane. It was produced in Finland during the following decade and served until the 1930s. **I.V.L. A22 Hansa** IL-2 is at the Finnish Aviation Museum, Helsinki in May 1998.

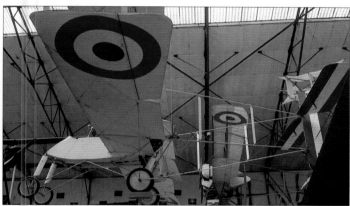

French manufacturer **Voisin** produced the **LA5-B2** pusher biplane. It served as a bomber in the early days of World War One and is seen in the charge of the Musée de l'Air, Paris, in June 1977.

The two-seat **Martinsyde F4 Buzzard** entered service too late for World War One, and saw limited RAF service. The type was sold in the early 1920s to the Finnish Air Force. MA-24 is on skis in its museum at Tikkakoski in June 1998.

Perhaps the most famous of all Royal Flying Corps fighters was the **Sopwith Camel**. N6812 is pictured, in February 1990, at the Imperial War Museum in London.

Original aeroplanes from World War One are rare, especially German ones. 101.40 is an **Aviatik D1**. Its survival was due to it being converted to a two-seater and hidden in a barn until 1976, after which it was restored to its former glory. It is seen at the Champlin Fighter Museum at Mesa, Arizona in October 1984.

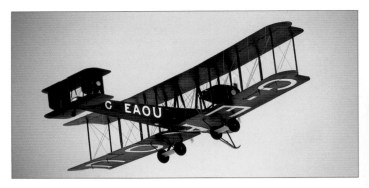

To re-create some of the epic flights of the **Vickers Vimy**, an RAF heavy bomber of World War One, a flying replica has been produced. NX71MY/G-EAOU is pictured at Fairford in July 1996. This aircraft flew to Australia from the UK, following the route of the first 1919 flight between the two countries.

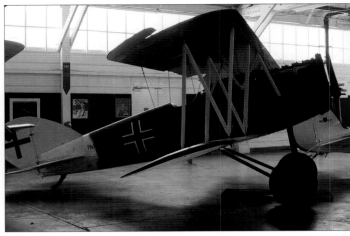

Above: When no real airframes are available, flying replicas are the best way to fill gaps in museums. N43C is a **Pfalz D.XII**, a fully airworthy copy of the 1918 German fighter. It is at the Champlin Fighter Museum in October 1984.

Left: The sole surviving example of its type is this **Breguet BR.273**. It was one of nine purchased by the Venezuelan Air Force from France in the 1930s. As can be seen, the top wing is much longer than the bottom. It is at Maracay in November 1992.

A design from the Royal Aircraft Factory, the **RE8** was a widely-used photo-reconnaissance and observation aircraft for the RFC and later the RAF. Seen in June 1983 is a Belgian example, No 8, in the Royal Army Museum, Brussels.

Used by the US Army Air Corps as an advanced trainer, the single-seat **Thomas-Morse S4C** was powered by an 80hp Le Rhône radial. N1115 is at the Cradle of Aviation Museum, Mitchel Field, Long Island in May 1989.

A French-designed World War One single-seat fighter, the **Nieuport 28C Bébé** was sold to the Swiss Air Force. 607 is displayed in its museum at Dubendorf in August 1987.

Entering service in 1918, the **Fokker D.VII** was one of the finest German World War One fighters. 6796/18 belongs to the Musée de l'Air and is pictured at the earlier location of Meudon in June 1977.

Left: The **Nieuport 17C** was a mid-World War One French single-seat fighter. Later use was as an advanced trainer. N5024 is seen in June 1983 at the Royal Army Museum, Brussels.

Below left: First introduced into German service in 1917, the **Albatros D.V** was a single-seat fighter powered by a Mercedes D.III liquid-cooled engine of either 180 or 200hp. 7161/17 is pictured in May 1989 at the National Air and Space Museum in Washington DC.

Below right: Powered by a 300hp Hispano-Suiza engine, the **Nieuport-Delage 29C** was a 1918 French single-seat fighter. No 010 is now at the Musée de l'Air in Paris, and is pictured when at Meudon in June 1977.

Above left: The **Sopwith 1½ Strutter** was the first British aircraft to arrive in service already equipped with synchronising gear to allow the machine-gun to fire through the blades of the propeller. S85 is a Belgian example at the Royal Army Museum, Brussels in June 1983.

Above right: In its original form the Avro 504 first appeared in 1913. Its role was that of an *ab initio* trainer. The last variant in RAF service, the 504K, soldiered on until the end of the 1920s. G-ADEV/H5199, marked as E3404, is an **Avro 504K** operated by the Shuttleworth Trust from Old Warden, where it is seen flying in April 1971.

Right: A single-seat fighter powered by an 80hp Le Rhône rotary engine, the **Sopwith Pup** served both the RFC and the RNAS. G-EBKY/N5180 is preserved in flying condition by the Shuttleworth Trust, and is pictured at its Old Warden base in July 1989.

Right: Entering RFC service in 1917, the **Bristol F2b Fighter** remained operational until 1932. A two-seater, it was powered by a 280hp Rolls-Royce Falcon. G-AEPH/D8096 is kept airworthy by the Shuttleworth Trust at Old Warden, where it is pictured in July 1989.

Below: The only authentic German aircraft of World War One to be found flying in the UK was the **LVG C.VI**. Designed as a two-seater observation aircraft, it is powered by a 200hp Benz Bz IV liquid-cooled engine. G-AANJ/7198/18 is pictured, in July 1989, at its Old Warden base in the hands of the Shuttleworth Trust.

Produced by the Royal Aircraft Factory, the **SE5a** entered service in the spring of 1917 with 56 Squadron. G-EBIA/F904 is preserved in flying condition by the Shuttleworth Trust and is pictured on a visit to Duxford in July 1994.

Above: In 1920 this **Macchi Telegrafo No 1** flew from Brazil to Quito in Ecuador. The design is an Italian-built Hanriot HD.1. Photographed in September 1997, it is the oldest airframe in the Ecuadorian Air Force Museum at Quito.

Below: The 1917-vintage French **SPAD 13 C.1** was powered by a 200hp Hispano-Suiza engine. More than 8,000 were built and the type was the mount of several French aces. SP-49 is in the Royal Army Museum, Brussels in June 1983.

Above: Flown by the Belgian Air Force during the campaign over Flanders, the **Hanriot HD.1** was a single-seat fighter. HD-78 is preserved, in period markings, at the Royal Army Museum, Brussels in June 1983.

Below: First flown in 1916, the French-built **SPAD S.7** was a single-seat fighter/scout biplane powered by a Hispano-Suiza engine of 140hp. B9913/S445 is pictured, in July 1986, in National Aviation Museum at Rockcliffe, Ontario.

A twin-engined bomber, the **AEG G.IV** 574/18, pictured in July 1986 at Canada's National Aviation Museum is the only multi-engined German aircraft of the period to survive. It could carry a bomb-load of 880 lb.

Above: The **Sopwith Snipe** was the RAF's replacement for the Camel. Powered by a Bentley BR.2 engine of 230hp, it entered service in September 1918. E6938 is seen in July 1986, displayed at the National Aviation Museum at Rockcliffe, Ontario.

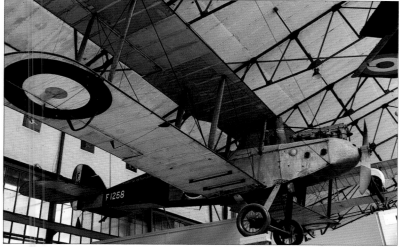

Left: A two-seat, single-engined day bomber, the **de Havilland DH.9** had a long career in the RAF. It entered service in 1918 and was withdrawn in 1931. F1258 is in the Musée de l'Air and is pictured when part of the museum was at Meudon in June 1977.

Below: A World War One bomber, the **Royal Aircraft Factory BE2C** had a poor record with the RFC on the Western Front in 1915, yet an RNAS machine destroyed a Zeppelin in 1916. 2699 is pictured at the Imperial War Museum, London in February 1990.

Above: The first biplane to loop, in 1913, the **Caudron G.3** was powered by an 80hp Le Rhône engine. More than 3,000 airframes were produced. 2531 is at the Royal Army Museum, Brussels in June 1983.

Right: The **Halberstadt C.V** was a two-seat photographic reconnaissance aircraft. It entered German service in the summer of 1918. 3471/18 is seen at the Royal Army Museum, Brussels in June 1983.

Left: Developed from the civil Cessna 337 Skymaster, the O-2 was an observation aircraft used by forward air controllers. It had two Continental 210hp piston engines, one as a pusher and the other as a tractor. **Cessna O-2A** VH-OTO/67-21431 is pictured, in February 2003, at Archer Field, Brisbane where it is operated as a privately-owned warbird.

Below: Still in daily worldwide use, the **de Havilland Canada DHC-2 Beaver** is a carry-anything, land-anywhere utility aircraft. FAC 108 is pictured in November 1992 at the Colombian Air Force Museum, Bogotá.

A design for an advanced trainer and COIN (counter-insurgency) aircraft that only reached the prototype stage was the **RTAF 5**. Produced in Thailand by the air force, the sole example is pictured, in November 1999, in its Bangkok museum.

Above: In the 1950s the search was on for a practical VTOL aircraft. One of the designs questing for this goal was the **Lockheed XFV-1**. It flew using a conventional undercarriage, but never vertically. 138657 is at the Sun 'n Fun Air Museum at Lakeland, Florida in April 1994.

Right: First flown in Spain in 1955, the **Dornier Do 27** went into production in Germany. Its role was as a light general-purpose transport, and the powerplant was a 270hp Lycoming. 57+56 is seen, in June 1983, preserved as a technical training airframe at the Luftwaffe base at Fassberg.

The **Westland Wyvern** was the last fixed-wing aircraft from the manufacturer. It was a single-seat, carrier-borne strike aircraft for the Royal Navy. Wyvern TF.1 VR137 is at the FAA Museum at Yeovilton in July 1994.

A light utility aircraft with an excellent short-field performance, the **Helio U-10A Super Courier** was used for many missions during the Vietnam War, including some by the CIA. 62-3606 is seen in October 1981 at Hurlburt Field, Florida.

Operated by the Yugoslavian Air Force until the early 1990s as a light attack aircraft, the **Soko J-20 Kraguj** had six underwing hardpoints for various weapons. Power was a single 340hp Lycoming. G-SOKO/30149 is a privately-owned example seen, in August 1995, at Liverpool-Speke Airport.

A primary trainer, the **Beech Musketeer** was used by the Canadian Armed Forces from 1981 to 1992. Its service designation was CT-134. Pictured, in September 2005, at the RCAF Museum, Trenton is 134213 in its bright training scheme.

Lockheed began work in 1966 to produce an ultra-quiet aircraft to track communist guerrillas in Vietnam. Following trials with converted sailplanes the **YO-3A** was produced for the US Army. N33YQ is a civil example, following retirement, and is pictured at Arlington, Washington in September 1984.

A carrier-borne fighter, the **Ryan FR-1 Fireball** had both a piston and a jet engine. A total of 66 were delivered to the US Navy starting in 1945. The type was withdrawn two years later after several carrier tours. 39709 is pictured, in October 1984, at the Fighter Jets & Air Racing Museum at Chino, California.

The first aircraft designed and built by Scottish Aviation was the **Pioneer CC.1**. It was a high-wing, single-engined utility aircraft with a very short take-off and landing performance. First flown in 1950, it served the RAF in many colonial operations. XL703/8034M is at the RAF Museum, Cosford in May 1993.

Above left: In the role of carrier-based attack aircraft, the **Martin AM-1 Mauler** had the largest available engine to lift its load – a 3,000hp P&W R-3350 radial piston. Although a success, the US Navy placed its main production order for the Skyraider. 122397 is at the US Navy Museum at Pensacola, Florida in April 1994.

Above right: Swiss manufacturer EKW (Eidg Konstruktions Werkstatte) produced the **C-3603** in 1939. It was a two-seat fighter-bomber. Power was from a single 1,000hp Hispano-Suiza liquid-cooled engine. Later roles included target-towing and some airframes were converted to turboprop power as the C-3605. Pictured in September 2004 at the Swiss Air Force Museum at Dubendorf is C-3603 C-534.

Left: Evaluated by the US Army for observation and liaison, the **Boeing YL-15** first flew in 1947. Production orders were not forthcoming. 47-429 is seen in October 1981 at the US Army Museum at Fort Rucker.

Two versions of the **Grumman Guardian** were produced. One was the AF-2W as a radar-equipped hunter and the other was the AF-2S in the killer role. One of each type would fly together on missions for the US Navy. N9993Z/126731 is in the latter configuration at the then Confederate Air Force's Arizona Wing HQ at Mesa in October 1998.

Used by the FAA first in the anti-submarine role and later as an airborne early-warning aircraft, the **Fairey Gannet** entered service in 1954 and flew until the end of the Royal Navy's traditional carrier operations. The type was exported to Australia, Indonesia and the German Navy. Pictured in May 1989, at the Midland Air Museum, Coventry is Gannet T.2 XA508/A2472.

The **Hawker Sea Fury** was the Royal Navy's last piston-engined fighter. It served in the front line for seven years from 1947, including operations in Korea where one destroyed a MiG-15. Pictured in February 2003, about to display at Avalon, Australia, is Sea Fury FB.10 VH-SHF/WJ232.

The Sea Fury has proved to be a popular warbird and is often raced because even 'stock' aircraft have a very high speed. **Sea Fury FB.11** N588 is seen rounding the pylons at Reno, Nevada, in September 1988.

To extend the already high performance of the **Sea Fury**, some special racers have had the Bristol Centaurus replaced with a P&W R-4360. NX4434P *Furias* is such a machine. It is pictured at an airshow at Madera, California in August 1986.

The **Douglas AD-1 Skyraider** provided the US military with one of its most versatile aircraft. Original operations were by the US Navy as both an attack bomber and AEW platform. A-1H 135300 is seen in October 1979 at the gate of Lemoore NAS, California.

Left: USAF operations of the **Douglas A-1 Skyraider** began during the Vietnam War when ex-Navy airframes were transferred for the role of ground-attack. They found fame in the role of supporting the helicopters that were sent to rescue pilots shot down in North Vietnam. A-1E 132463 is pictured, in October 2001, at the McClellan Museum in California.

Right: With the large numbers of airframes available, the **Skyraider** has become a popular warbird with collectors. AD-4NA G-RAID/126922 is a privately-owned UK machine pictured at Duxford in July 1994.

Below: British use of the Skyraider was with the Fleet Air Arm as a three-seat, carrier-borne, radar-equipped early-warning aircraft. It served until 1960, becoming the last fixed-wing, piston-powered aircraft in front-line service. **Skyraider AEW.1** WT121 is pictured, in July 1994, at the FAA Museum, Yeovilton.

The **Commonwealth CA-16 Wirraway** was an Australian-licensed development of the T-6 Texan/Harvard. Power was from a 600hp P&W Wasp air-cooled radial engine. First flown in March 1939, production continued until 1946. VH-WIR/A20-652 is a privately-owned warbird pictured, in February 2003, at Avalon, Victoria.

Preserved up a pole, in November 1992, at the Bolivian Air Force base at Santa Cruz is **PT-17 Stearman** FAB 007. The air arm keeps another airworthy for pilots to enjoy.

Peru also operated the **PT-17 Stearman**. Pictured in September 1997 at the air force museum at Las Palmas, Lima is 126.

For airshow acts in the USA some Stearmans have been re-engined with powerplants as big as 450hp P&W R-985s: the basic unit for the type is a 220hp Continental. N49603 is a **Super Stearman** so converted for the airshow performer Earl Cherry. Note the wing-walker on the top. It is seen flying at Biggs AAF, Texas in October 1984.

First produced in Canada, the **DHC-1 Chipmunk** served with the RAF in a number of training roles ending with the University Air Squadrons and Air Experience Flights. Following their service careers they have proved to be popular private machines. G-AOTD/WB588 is pictured displaying at Old Warden in July 1989.

Above left: Following its first flight in 1945, the **Yakovlev Yak-18** (*Max*) has developed from a basic trainer into a whole family of aircraft. 621 is an Egyptian Air Force example seen, in June 1988, at the Military Museum in Cairo.

Above right: The Yak-18 has been produced in China and further developed. **Nanchang CJ-6** '34 white' is pictured at the Guangzhou Technical Institute in use as a training airframe in October 1999. Note the different tail from the original Russian design.

Left: A rugged two-seat tandem trainer, the **Pilatus P.2** was designed to operate from high-altitude airfields. It first flew in 1945 and served the Swiss Air Force. G-BJAX/J-108 is a privately-owned example seen at Mildenhall in May 1982.

Czechoslovakia has produced some of the best aerobatic aircraft in the world. These have evolved from the 1947-designed **Zlin 226 Trener**. This type has been used for both civil and military training. The illustrated example is in the Military Museum, Cairo in June 1988.

Above: First flown in 1962, the **PZL-104 Wilga** (Thrush) is a Polish general-purpose light aircraft. Its roles include agriculture, glider-towing, parachuting and club flying. 254 is an Egyptian Air Force example pictured at the Military Museum, Cairo in June 1988.

Left: Fully aerobatic, the **SIAI-Marchetti SF.260** is a trainer and touring aircraft in the civil market place. Military versions use it both for flying and weapons training as it can be fitted with wing hardpoints for ordnance. SF.260MS 123 is pictured, in February 2003, the Republic of Singapore Air Force Museum.

A four-seat primary trainer, the **Saab 91 Safir** dates back to 1945. Following military service it has found its way onto the private market. OH-SFJ is an ex-Finnish Air Force example and is seen at an airshow at Tampere in June 1998.

Above: Built by Fokker in Holland as a two-seat primary trainer, the **S.11 Instructor** first flew in 1947 and served in the Dutch military until 1973. Pictured in October 2003 at the gate of the National Institute of Civil Aviation in Asuncion, Paraguay is ZP-EAC.

Right: Originally used by the RAF as a basic trainer, the **Percival Prentice** did not serve for long. A few airframes were converted for civil use but the 250hp de Havilland Gipsy Queen engine is small for the size of airframe, making it underpowered. G-APJB/VR259 is preserved in flying condition by Air Atlantique at Coventry, where it is pictured in August 1999.

One of the most popular flying club basic trainers, the **Cessna 150** has had some sales in the military field. FAE 00506 is a retired example, seen in September 1997 at the Ecuadorian Air Force Museum at Quito.

A tandem two-seat advanced trainer, the **Soko Type 522** is a Yugoslavian design powered by a P&W R-1340 600hp radial engine. It entered service in 1957. NX121DV/60121 is privately-owned and seen at Scottsdale, Arizona in October 1998.

Left: A deck-landing version of an RAF two-seat advanced trainer, the **Boulton Paul Sea Balliol T.21** was powered by a Rolls-Royce Merlin of 1,280hp. WL732 is pictured in May 1993 at the RAF Museum, Cosford.

Right: Used by the USAAF as a basic trainer, the **Fairchild PT-23** was one of a number of variations on the same basic type. This one had open cockpits and was powered by a 220hp Continental air-cooled radial engine. N49272 is pictured in August 1989 at an airshow at West Malling, Kent.

Below: First flown in 1939, the **Vultee BT-13 Valiant** was a tandem two-seat basic trainer powered by a 450hp P&W R-985 air-cooled engine. NC58566 is seen in August 1986 at an airshow at Madera, California.

A conversion of a Harvard by the E L Bacon Corp of Santa Monica in the mid-1950s produced the **Bacon Super T-6**. It has a new engine, tip-tanks, a one-piece canopy and a tricycle undercarriage. N66J is seen in October 1984 at Whitman, California.

The Pacific Aerospace Company in New Zealand produced the **CT-4 Airtrainer**; this aircraft had its roots in the Australian Victa Airtourer. The RAAF used it as a basic trainer and since then they have been sold as surplus to the civil market. VH-CTK is a privately-owned example, pictured in February 2003 at Avalon, Victoria. It still wears its RAAF markings.

Above: The Army Air Corps used the Auster range for many years in the liaison and observation roles. **Auster AOP.5** G-AKOW/TJ569 is in its Middle Wallop museum in July 1984.

Left: Nearly 3,000 airframes of the **Cessna O-1 Bird Dog** were produced for the US Army. Its roles included liaison, observation and flight training. 51-11989 is seen, in July 1984, at the Museum of Army Flying at Middle Wallop on loan from the US Army.

Developed from the O-1 Bird Dog was the **Cessna 185/U-17**; its roles were similar. 755 is a gate guard at the Uruguayan Air Force base at Durazno in October 2003.

Becoming the RAF's standard basic trainer in 1953, the **Percival Provost T.1** was powered by a 550hp Alvis Leonides radial engine. Its last service role was with the Central Air Traffic Control School in 1969. G-BKHP/WW397 is a privately-owned example seen at an airshow at Liverpool-Speke in August 1984.

Australia built the **Commonwealth CA-25 Winjeel** (Eagle) for the same role as the Percival Provost. Power was from a 445hp P&W Wasp air-cooled radial engine. Now surplus, they can be found with private owners. VH-WJE/A85-427 still wears its dayglo at Avalon, Victoria, in February 2003.

Beech developed the **T-34 Mentor** from the popular Bonanza. A two-seat tandem primary trainer, it was powered by a 225hp Continental engine. Widely exported, a turboprop version still serves with the US Navy. 685 is a Uruguayan example, seen in October 2003 at the gate of the air base at Durazno.

Above left: Developed from the Yak-3 fighter, the **Yakovlev Yak-11** (*Moose*) is an advanced trainer. First flown in 1946, it has been widely exported to communist bloc countries and their allies. '25 yellow' is seen in the Yakovlev museum, Moscow, in August 1991.

Above right: With a 730hp Shvetsov ASh-21 radial engine, the **Yak-11** gives the private pilot a very high-performance two-seater. G-BTUB is pictured, in July 1994, in bogus military markings at Duxford.

Left: First in service with the USAF and then the US Navy, the **North American T-28 Trojan** has been widely exported in its role as a basic trainer for military pilots. T-28B FAB 411 is a Bolivian Air Force example pictured, in November 1992, at El Trompillo Air Force Base, Santa Cruz.

Above left: The **Curtiss 68 Hawk III** was an export version of the BF2C-1 fighter-bomber operated by the US Navy. It was one of the few biplanes to have a retractable undercarriage. In the late summer of 1934 Siam, now Thailand, purchased twelve. The last survivor of the type is pictured, in November 1989, in the Bangkok museum.

Above right: USN **T-28B Trojans** differed in having a more powerful engine: a Wright R-1820 of 1,425hp. The T-28C had an added arrester hook to practise deck landings. N311LK/146253 is in private hands; in USMC markings, it is seen at Lakeland, Florida, in April 1994.

Right: The **T-28D Trojan** was developed for low-budget counter-insurgency operations. It had wing hardpoints for various weapons stores. VH-TRO is a privately-owned example operated from Archerfield, Brisbane in February 2003.

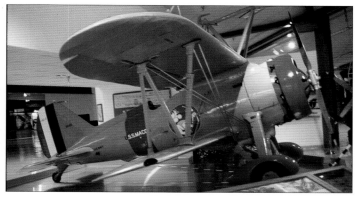

Above left: Despite losing a contest to supply the USAAC with a fighter, the **Curtiss 75 Hawk** sold well in the world marketplace. There were versions with both fixed and retractable undercarriages. One of the former is seen, in November 1999, in the RTAF Museum, Bangkok.

Above right: Designed as a hook-on fighter for the US Navy's rigid airships, the **Curtiss F9C-2 Sparrowhawk** first flew in 1931. A9058 bears the name of the airship USS *Macon* at the Pensacola museum, Florida in April 1994.

Left: Curtiss produced the **F7C-1 Seahawk** for a 1927 navy fighter competition. Powered by a single 450hp P&W R-1340 engine, it served only with the US Marine Corps. A7667 is pictured in the Corps' markings at Pensacola, Florida in April 1994.

Right: Used by the US Navy as a fighter-trainer, the **Curtiss SNC-1 Falcon** was powered by a 420hp Wright Whirlwind R-975 air-cooled engine. 05194 is seen, in April 1994, suspended in the Pensacola museum.

Below left: A two-seat observation aircraft for the US Army, the **Curtiss O-52 Owl** was first flown in 1941. It had a short service life. 40-2763 is pictured, in July 1986, at the USAF Museum, Dayton, Ohio.

Below right: The **Grumman F3F-2** was the last biplane fighter in any of the US armed services. It was developed from the F2F-1 with the installation of a larger 950hp Wright R-1820 radial engine. 0976 is in USMC markings at the Pensacola museum, Florida, in April 1994.

Used by Gulf Oil as a promotional tool, a single **Grumman G-22 Gulfhawk II**, NR1050, was produced. It was basically an amalgam of the F2F-1 and the F3F-2. First flown in 1936, it was used by the aerobatic pilot Al Williams until 1948 when it was presented to the NASM, where it was pictured in May 1989.

Procured as a utility amphibian, the **Grumman J2F Duck** had a large fuselage float. It entered operations with the USN in 1934 and served with the USCG and USAF until the beginning of the 1950s. N1214N/33549 is owned by the Fantasy of Flight Museum at Polk City, Florida. It is pictured at Lakeland in April 2005.

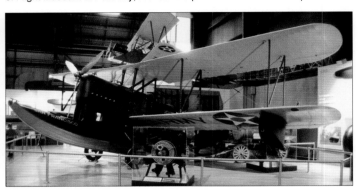

The first Vought Corsair dates from 1927 with the 02U-1. The design was sold to Siam (Thailand) in two forms, one as complete aircraft and the other under licensed production. **V93S Corsair** 14682 is one of the latter, and the sole survivor of the type in the world. It is at the Bangkok museum in November 1999.

Used by both the USAAC and the US Navy, the **Loening OA-1A** was an observation monoplane powered by a 400hp Liberty V-1650 engine and flown by a crew of two. 26-431 is in the USAF Museum at Dayton in July 1986.

Above left: The **Douglas O-38**, an observation biplane, was powered by a 525hp P&W R-1690 engine. Last use of the type was by the Air National Guard in training and target-tug roles up to 1942. 33-324 is at the USAF Museum in July 1986.

Above right: A high-wing, two-crew observation aircraft for the USAAC, the **Douglas O-46A** was the final development of a line that started with the XO-31. The powerplant was a 725hp P&W R-1535. 35-179 is seen in July 1986, suspended at the USAF Museum.

Left: From the Northrop A-17 attack bomber Douglas developed the model 8 for export. Ordered in 1938 for the Peruvian Air Force under the designation **Douglas DB8A-3P** the type soldiered on until the late 1950s. Sole survivor XXX1-1 is pictured, in October 2003, at the gate of the Air Force Academy, Las Palmas, Lima.

Left: Pictured in September 2002 at Madrid's Museo del Aire is this Spanish Civil War-vintage **Fiat CR.32** 3-52. During the 1930s this Italian manufacturer had produced a number of biplane fighters starting with the CR.30 and culminating with the World War Two CR.42, all were renowned for their manoeuvrability.

Below left: The **North American O-47B** was a single-engine observation aircraft powered by a 975hp Wright R-1820 radial piston engine. First flown in 1938, its main service career was in second-line duties. N4725Y is seen in October 1979, owned by Planes of Fame at Chino, California.

Below right: The **Curtiss NC4** flying-boat, A2294, was the first to fly the Atlantic; it did so, however, in four stages and took from the 8th to 31st May 1919. It is seen at Pensacola in October 1981.

Above left: One of a number of specialist racing aircraft of the 1930s, the **Caudron C366** No 01 is pictured, in May 1983, at the Musée de l'Air, Paris.

Above right: A single-seat fighter powered by a 435hp Curtiss D12 engine, the **Boeing FB-5** served both the USN and USMC. A7114 is at the Corps' Museum at Quantico, Virginia in May 1989.

Right: Pictured at the RAF Museum in December 1977 is 920, a **Supermarine Stranraer**. This airframe was one of a number built in Canada by Canadian Vickers under licence. Its role was maritime reconnaissance.

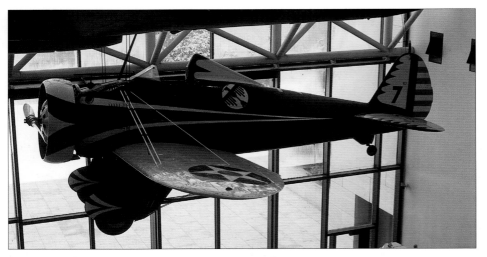

Left: Boeing's P-26 achieved two firsts. It was the first monoplane fighter in production for the USAAC, and it was also its first all-metal fighter. 33-135 is at the NASM in Washington DC in May 1989.

Below left: The survivor of a pair of **Boeing 100Es** purchased by the RTAF is seen on show at its museum in Bangkok in November 1999. This model was a single-seat fighter for export or commercial use, based on the F4B-1.

Below right: In the mid-1930s the Argentine Navy purchased three Canadian-built **Fairchild 82Ds** equipped for high-altitude photography. The sole survivor, LV-FHZ, is pictured in October 2003 at the Argentine national museum at Moron.

Above left: The world's last 'real' **Bristol Bulldog** is this Finnish example, BU-59. It is seen in June 1998 at the Hallinportti Aviation Museum. The Finns purchased seventeen in 1934 and they flew operations against the Russians in 1939.

Above right: Frenchman Pierre Latécoère, in 1918, formed Aéropostale to connect his native land with South America. **Latécoère 25** F-AIEH is the restored prototype and sole survivor of a fleet of eleven. The airmail routes were amongst the most dangerous and remote of all time. In his book *Wind, Sand and Stars* the great French writer and pilot Antoine de Saint-Exupéry describes such flights. This aircraft is on display at the national collection at Moron, Buenos Aires and is pictured there in October 2003.

Right: A single-seat fighter development from the Harvard, the **North American NA-50** was sold to Peru in small numbers. 50-951/3-41 is pictured in October 2003 at the gate of the Las Palmas base, Lima.

The Hawker Hart spawned a huge family of variants and sub-types for British and foreign air forces. The Demon was a two-seat fighter first flown in 1932 and powered by a single Rolls-Royce Kestrel liquid-cooled engine. **Hawker Demon 1** A1-8 is pictured at the RAAF Museum, Point Cook, Victoria, in February 2003.

In the 1930s Hawker produced a whole family of elegant biplanes from the Hart. One variant was an advanced trainer. It had tandem seating and was powered by a single Rolls-Royce Kestrel engine. This was the **Hart Trainer**. K4972/1764M is seen at the RAF Museum, Cosford in May 1993.

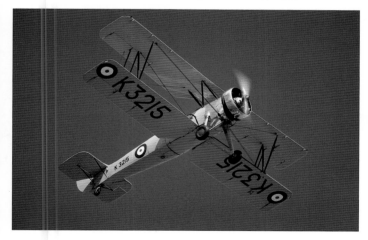

Above: A two-seat elementary trainer, the **Avro Tutor** was chosen in 1932 to replace the Avro 504. G-AHSA/K3215 is owned by the Shuttleworth Trust and can be found flying at a limited number of airshows. It is pictured here at Fairford in July 1995.

Right: A general-purpose light day bomber, the **Hawker Hind** was another in the line derived from the Hart. The powerplant in this two-seater was the Rolls-Royce Kestrel of 640hp. G-AENP/K5415 was recovered from Afghanistan in the 1960s and flew for some years in its air force markings. Owned by the Shuttleworth Trust it is seen at Old Warden, in July 1998, in the period RAF markings of XV (15) Squadron.

A French high-wing fighter of the 1920s, the **Gourdou-Leseurre GL22** was operated by the Finnish Air Force on both wheels and skis. Sole survivor 8F-12 is pictured, in June 1998, in the air force museum at Tikkakoski.

Above: Restored to flying condition in 1982, OH-XGT/GT-400 is the only airworthy **Gloster Gauntlet** in the world. A single-seat fighter, it first flew in 1933, entering RAF service two years later. Finland received 25 ex-RAF machines in 1940, and this last example is seen at an airshow in Tampere in June 1998.

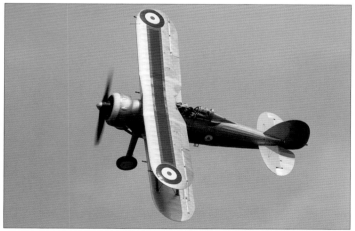

The **Gloster Gladiator**, last of the RAF's biplane fighters, saw extensive front-line service in World War Two. Powered by an 840hp Bristol Mercury engine, it entered service in 1937. G-AMRK/L8032 is kept in flying condition by the Shuttleworth Trust at Old Warden, where it is pictured flying in July 1989.

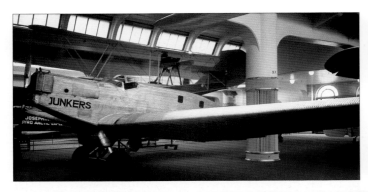

Above left: Junkers W33 D1167 was the first aircraft to fly the east-west route across the Atlantic when, in 1928, it flew from Ireland to Labrador. A single-engine, all-metal light transport monoplane, it had a Junkers L5 liquid-cooled engine. It is pictured, in July 1986, at the Henry Ford Museum, Dearborn, Michigan.

Above right: South America was a well-known trading partner with Germany during the 1920s and 1930s. **Junkers W34s** were operated by SCADTA, a joint Colombian-German airline, together with the Colombian Air Force. Nine aircraft were obtained in 1932 and they served for twenty years. FAC 407 is pictured at the Bogotá museum in November 1992.

Left: Whereas the Junkers W33 had a liquid-cooled engine, the **Junkers W34** had an air-cooled one; many different units were fitted. CF-ATF is a Canadian example pictured, in July 1986, at the National Aviation Museum, Rockcliffe, Ontario.

Above left: A four-seat, low-wing cabin monoplane, the **Messerschmitt Bf 108 Taifun** (Typhoon) first flew in 1934. It was widely used as a liaison aircraft during World War Two and a version was built in France following the war. A-201 is an ex-Swiss Air Force example and is pictured in August 1987, preserved within the terminal at Zurich-Kloten Airport.

Above right: The **Dewoitine D27** was a French high-wing fighter of the late 1920s. F-AZJA/290 is an airworthy example seen in July 1997 visiting an airshow at Duxford.

Right: Pictured in September 1984, at Snohomish-Harvey, Washington, is a privately-owned **Howard DGA-15**, NC52947. This was a four/five-seat cabin monoplane that served in the US Army as the UC-70 and in the US Navy as the NH-1.

Above left: Handley Page designed the **HP.39 Gugnunc** for a 1927 American competition to produce a 'safe' aeroplane. The name is derived from 'Guggenheim Competition Biplane'. Only one was produced and G-AACN is pictured in September 1983 at Wroughton, the Science Museum outstation.

Above right: An ultra-light design, the **Mignet HM.14 Pou-de-Ciel** (Flying Flea) was produced in France during the 1930s and by many builders in their own homes. It had a poor safety record. OH-BFA is in the Finnish Aviation Museum, Helsinki in May 1998.

Right: A single-seat racing monoplane, the **Percival P.6 Mew Gull** won the King's Cup Air Race in 1938. It has had a number of different powerplants during its life. G-AEXF is pictured in July 1982, flying at Cranfield. It is now owned by the Shuttleworth Trust.

The **Noorduyn Norseman** is one of the great workhorse aircraft of Canada. First flown in 1935, it can still be found operating on wheels, skis, or floats in the backwoods. CF-SAN is preserved in flying condition by the owner of Buffalo Airways at Yellowknife, North West Territories in May 2000.

A two-seat, side-by-side cabin monoplane, the **Aeronca C-3** first flew in 1934. Its engines varied from a 40 to a 65hp unit. G-AEFT is seen at Cranfield in July 1982.

A military variant of the Vega Gull, the **Percival Proctor** saw extensive RAF service in the communications and radio-training roles. After the war many surplus machines found their way onto the civil register. P.30 Proctor II G-ALJF is pictured visiting Cranfield in July 1987.

In 1947 the Belgian Air Force received six ex-RAF **Percival P.31 Proctor IVs**. They were used for three years in a communications role. P4 is pictured, in June 1983, at the Royal Army Museum, Brussels.

Above: Powered by a 62hp Walter Mikron air-cooled engine, the Belgian-designed **Tipsy B** was a side-by-side, two-seat trainer dating from 1937. G-AISB is seen visiting Cranfield in July 1982.

Below: A five-seat cabin touring aircraft with a high wing, the **Cessna 195** was produced between 1947 and 1954, nearly 1,000 airframes being constructed. JA3007 is pictured, in October 2004, at the Museum of Aeronautical Science at Narita Airport, Tokyo.

Right: An amphibian of all-metal construction, the powerplant of the **Fleetwing Seabird** is mounted over the top of the wing. NC16793 is seen at Oshkosh in August 1986.

Below: A Brazilian designed and built trainer, the **Neiva N.621 Universal (T-25)** has been sold to a number of South American countries. The manufacturer has since been taken over by Embraer. Pictured in October 2003 at Paraguay's Nhu Guazu Air Force Base as a gate guard is T-25 0125.

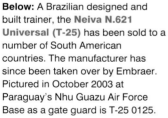

Belgian-designed, the **Stampe SV.4** has been produced in its home country as well as in France. First flown in 1933, it is a two-seat primary trainer. G-FORC is pictured at Cranfield in July 1987.

Produced in 1938, the **Harlow PJC-2** was a four-place cabin monoplane powered by a Warner-Scarab air-cooled radial engine. N3947B is at Oshkosh in August 1986.

The Auster company in Britain produced a whole family of high-wing touring and training aircraft. **J/5F Aiglet Trainer** G-AMRF is at Cranfield in July 1982. This variant was the first fully aerobatic model and was powered by a 130hp de Havilland Gipsy Major engine.

Left: First flown in 1934, the **Bücker Bü 131B Jungmann** was a two-seat aerobatic biplane with a Hirth air-cooled engine. A-67 is an ex-Swiss Air Force example pictured, in August 1987, within the terminal at Zurich-Kloten Airport.

Below: Following the Jungmann into the air a year later came the **Bücker Bü 133C Jungmeister**. Again its role was aerobatics but this had just a single seat and a radial engine. N133BU is at the Virginia Aviation Museum, Richmond, in May 1989.

1935 saw the Venezuelan Air Force buy three **Morane-Saulnier MS.147s** from France. These were used as trainers. 012 is at the air force museum at Maracay in November 1992.

Designed by the racing pilot Roscoe Turner and built by the Lawrence W Brown Aircraft Company in California, the **Turner RT-14 Meteor** won the Thompson Trophy race in both 1938 and 1939. NX263Y is on show at the NASM Silver Hill site, Maryland in May 1989. It has since moved to the new Udvar-Hazy Center at Washington-Dulles Airport.

Above: Designed as a high-performance mail and people-carrier, the **Northrop Alpha** had an open cockpit for the pilot but an enclosed cabin for the passengers. It was powered by a 420hp P&W Wasp engine. NC11Y is on display at the NASM, Washington DC in May 1989.

Right: In 1936 Consolidated asked Fleet in Canada to produce ten of their Model 21 trainers to fulfil an order for Mexico. This **Fleet 21M** was an eleventh airframe, built as a demonstrator. CF-DLC still flies and is seen in June 1990, owned by the Canadian Warplane Heritage at Hamilton, Ontario.

Above left: Pictured at San Bernadino, Paraguay in October 2003 is this privately-owned and flown but unregistered **Fleet 10/16**. The 10 was built with spruce and the 16 with Douglas fir. It is unclear what materials have been used during its restoration.

Above right: The **Lockheed Vega** achieved many world aviation firsts, not least the Wiley Post and Harold Gatty round-the-world trip in 1931. N965Y is pictured, in July 1986, at the Henry Ford Museum, Dearborn.

Left: One of the most widely-produced aircraft of all time was the **Polikarpov Po-2** (*Mule*). In production from 1928 to 1951, the total run was more than 33,000 airframes. With such a vast number, the roles it played were legion, from training and glider-towing to light attack. F-AZDB is in Yugoslavian markings as part of the Salis collection at La Ferté Alais in May 1983.

Right: A single-engined airliner powered by a 1,000hp Wright R-1850 radial, the **Vultee V-1A** was also used as an executive transport. NC16099 is seen, in May 1989, at the Virginia Aviation Museum in Richmond. This aeroplane had been owned by newspaper tycoon Randolph Hearst.

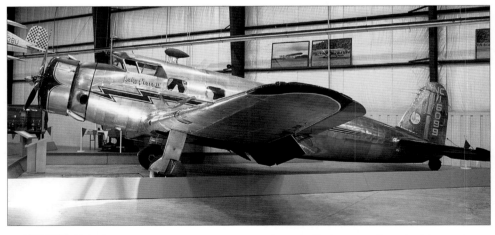

Below: The **Dart G** was a side-by-side cabin monoplane. Production began in 1938. NC20401 is pictured on a visit to Lakeland, Florida in April 1994.

Powered by a 65hp Continental air-cooled engine, the **Luscombe 8A Silvaire** first flew in 1937. G-AFZN is pictured at Cranfield in July 1982.

A four-seat cabin monoplane, the **Chrislea CH.3 Super Ace** first flew in 1946. A British aircraft, it was powered by a 145hp de Havilland Gipsy Major. G-AKVF is pictured at Cranfield in July 1982.

A very smart two-seat, side-by-side cabin monoplane, the **Pasped Skylark** first flew in 1936. The sole survivor is NC14919 and it is powered by a 175hp Super Scarab radial engine. It is photographed at Oshkosh, Wisconsin in August 1986.

The **Focke-Wulf Fw 44J Stieglitz**, a two-seat primary trainer, was produced under licence in Brazil, Sweden and Argentina as well as in its native Germany. D-EDYV is a private German example and is pictured on a visit to Fassberg in June 1983.

Above: The US Navy had its own design and manufacturing unit at the Philadelphia Navy Yard. The **N3N-3** was a primary trainer powered by a 235hp Wright R-760 radial engine. N45042/2582 is pictured in USCG markings in October 1979, attending an airshow at Travis AFB, California.

Below: First produced in 1932, the **Beech 17** 'Staggerwing' was a four-seat biplane with a retractable undercarriage. The powerplant was a 450hp P&W R-985 radial. N44G is seen, in August 1986, at Oshkosh, Wisconsin.

Above: The **Kreutzer K5 Air Coach**, a six-place tri-motor, was built in 1929. Powerplants were three 100hp Kinners. Of the fifteen built N612A is the last. It is pictured at Camarillo, California, in September 1988, following its return after forty-five years in Mexico.

Left: A post-war cabin monoplane, the **North American L-17 Navion** was used by the US Army and the Air National Guard for liaison duties. N5382K, in private ownership, is seen in military markings at Lakeland, Florida in April 1994.

Above left: The **Yakovlev Yak UT-1/Air-14** was a fighter-trainer dating from 1936. The first prototype is pictured, in August 1991, in the Yakovlev Museum, Moscow.

Above right: From the same design bureau came the **Yakovlev Yak UT-2** (*Mink*). This was a two-place basic trainer that had a production run of more than 7,000 airframes. No 3 is in the manufacturer's museum in Moscow in August 1991.

Left: With a production run from 1932 to 1936, the **Blackburn B2** was a side-by-side, two-seat basic trainer powered by a 130hp de Havilland Gipsy Major engine. Sole airworthy survivor G-AEBJ is owned by BAE Systems (which is a direct successor to the original manufacturer) and is kept at its Brough site. It is pictured in September 1989 on a visit to Finningley.

Right: Photographed, in May 2000, in airworthy condition at Fairbanks, Alaska, is this **Curtiss Wright Travel Air** N9966. It is now fitted with floats; note too, the extension below the rudder.

Below left: Designed for the Cranwell Light Aeroplane Club in 1929, the **Comper CLA 7 Swift** was a single-seat, high-wing monoplane. A total of 41 airframes were built and a number of different powerplants fitted. G-ACTF is pictured at Cranfield in July 1982.

Below right: A two-seat, side-by-side touring high-wing monoplane, the Monocoupe had a production run split by the war. There were three basic versions with different horsepower engines, a 60, 90 and 110. This **Monocoupe 110**, N36Y, was a specially modified racer fitted with a 185hp Warner Super Scarab. It won post-war air races and aerobatic events. It is now preserved in the Virginia Aviation Museum at Richmond, where it is seen in May 1989.

Above left: Powered by a single 150hp Menasco air-cooled engine the **Ryan STM** was an export version of the PT-16/20 for the Netherlands East Indies. VH-AWG is a privately owned Australian example pictured, in February 2003, at Tyabb, Victoria. It wears the Dutch military markings of the period.

Above right: The **Aircoupe**, a two-seat, side-by-side light touring aircraft, dates back to 1937. Its manufacturing rights have been held by several companies over the years. CP-697 is a privately-owned example at Santa Cruz, Bolivia in November 1992.

Right: Seating six, the **Bellanca CH-300** was used as a small airliner as well as the basis for record flights. NX237, originally a CH-300, has been converted to a CH-400 by changing the engine to a 450hp P&W and painting it in the markings of *Columbia,* the aircraft that flew from New York to Berlin in 1927 just days after the Lindbergh solo crossing to Paris. It is pictured, in May 1989, in the Virginia Aviation Museum, Richmond.

Above left: A two-seat club trainer and tourer, the **Avro Avian** dates back to 1926. The powerplant depended on the model. CF-CDV is at the Reynolds Museum, Alberta in May 2000.

Above right: Production deliveries of the **Convair L-13** started in 1947. Its role was as a general purpose and observation monoplane and it was powered by a 245hp Franklin O-425. N275LG/47-275 is a privately-owned example pictured at Lakeland, Florida, in April 1994.

Left: Only one example of the **English Electric Wren** survives. It was a single-seat, ultra-light monoplane. The engine was a 398cc ABC motor-cycle unit. No 4/BAPC 11 is owned by the Shuttleworth Trust and is pictured at its Old Warden base in July 1989.

Designed as a twin-engined pilot trainer, only one example of the **Reid & Sigrist RS4 Desford** was produced. First flown in 1945, it operated as a photographic survey aircraft using its glass nose. G-AGOS/VZ728 is pictured, in September 1977, when it was part of the Strathallan collection. It is now at the Snibston Discovery Park.

The idea of having an aeroplane that could be converted for road use resulted in the **Taylor Aerocar I** in the late 1940s. It had a 143hp Lycoming with a pusher propeller and the wings and tail were detachable. N100D is seen on show at the Museum of Flight at Boeing Field, Washington in May 2000.

First produced in 1929, the **New Standard D25** was a five-place biplane. It had two cockpits, one in the rear for the pilot and one in the front for the four passengers sitting in pairs. Power was from a 200hp Wright R-760 radial. NC903V is seen providing pleasure flights at Lakeland in April 1994.

Above: A licence-built version of the Klemm Kl.25, the **BA Swallow II** first flew in 1935. A two-seat touring and training aircraft, it had different powerplants in various models. G-AEVZ is pictured visiting Coventry in August 2000.

Below: The **Piper PA-18 Super Cub** can trace its roots back to the J-2 Cub of 1936. Cubs have been produced in the thousands and can be found with many private owners or clubs. OO-FLW is seen on a visit to Cranfield in July 1982.

Above: The American Waco company used three letters to designate the engine fit to the different model series. An -F series, the **Waco UPF-7** was a two-seat primary trainer introduced in 1937 and powered by a 220hp Continental W670 radial. G-WACO is photographed at Cranfield in July 1987.

Right: Known originally as the Stinson O-74, the **Vultee L-1 Vigilant** took its new name following the take-over of Stinson. First flown in 1940, it was an army co-operation aircraft with short take-off and landing performance. N704E is seen in October 1979 at Santa Susana, California.

Above left: A light amphibian with a single 85hp Walter radial, the **Shavrov Sh-1** was the first aircraft from that manufacturer in Russia. The design dates from 1928. CBC 28002 is pictured flying at Zhukovsky in August 1995.

Above right: The 'M' in the **Douglas M-2** stood for mail. It operated on early postal flights around parts of the USA. NC150 is in the NASM, Washington DC, in May 1989, in the livery of Western Air Express, which started operations in 1926 between Los Angeles and Salt Lake City.

Right: Introduced in 1931, the **Curtiss CW-15 Sedan** was a four-seat cabin monoplane. Prototype N436W is seen at Snohomish-Harvey, Washington in September 1984 being used as a jump aircraft for sports parachutists.

Above left: First flown in 1928, the **Curtiss Robin** was a three-seat cabin monoplane. It set a number of records including that of the world refuelling endurance of 653 hours, 34 minutes in 1935. NX979K is pictured, in May 2000, in the Museum of Flight, Boeing Field, Washington.

Above right: Pictured at Ciudad Bolivar in central Venezuela in November 1992 is **Ryan G2-W Flamingo** NC9487. It was in this aircraft in 1937, while looking for gold, that American pilot Jimmy Angel 'discovered' the world's tallest waterfall. A total of 3,212ft high, it was named Angel Falls after him.

Right: Two-seat trainer, the **Curtiss JN-4 Jenny** dates from 1916. It was used post-World War One for many barnstorming flights. N5001 is seen in period markings at Madera, California in August 1986.

The **Stinson Reliant** had two major versions. First was the straight-wing and then in 1936, the gull-wing series. The type was used during World War Two as a utility transport. NC731M, a second-series V-77 Reliant, is pictured in September 1997 in the Ecuadorian Air Force Museum at Quito.

Stinson SM-1 Detroiter NC857, the second to be produced, is pictured, in July 1986, at the Henry Ford Museum, Dearborn. This airframe made a flight from Newfoundland, across Europe to Japan in 1927.

In 1939 Stinson produced the **105 Voyager**, a three-seat cabin monoplane powered by a 75hp Continental. C-FBSU/3469 is pictured with the Canadian Warplane Heritage collection at Hamilton, Ontario in June 1990.

A primary trainer first flown in 1939, the **Fairchild Cornell** came in several versions. The PT-19 was the first and was powered by a 175hp Ranger air-cooled engine. This example is in the Venezuelan Air Force Museum at Maracay in November 1992.

Left: For training in the harsh Canadian winter, an enclosed cockpit was added to the **Fairchild Cornell**. This was designated PT-26B and the powerplant upgraded to a 200hp Ranger. C-GCWC/10835 is in period markings with the Canadian Warplane Heritage collection at Hamilton in June 1990.

Below: A two-seat primary trainer, the **Ryan PT-22** was introduced in 1940 having been developed from the STM range. It was widely used and proved post-war to be a popular light aircraft. N49049 is pictured flying at Oshkosh in August 1986.

Pictured in May 1989 is one of the most famous and historic aircraft in the NASM collection in Washington DC. NX211, a **Ryan NYP**, is better known as the *Spirit of St. Louis*. It is, of course, the aircraft in which Charles Lindbergh made the first solo crossing of the Atlantic Ocean in 1927.

A four-seat cabin monoplane that first flew in 1932, the **Fairchild 24** could be found with either an inline air-cooled engine or a radial. It saw military service as a general communications aircraft with the RAF as the Argus, and with the USAAF as the UC-61A. 7/94 is a Warner radial-engined version in the RTAF Museum, Bangkok in November 1989.

From the Miles M.2 Hawk came a number of different variants. **M.2R Hawk Major** CC-FBB is a two-seat trainer and is pictured, in October 2003, at the national collection of Chile at Los Cerrillos, Santiago.

A twin-engined touring aircraft, the **Miles M.65 Gemini** first flew in October 1945. G-AKKB is powered by a pair of 100hp Blackburn Cirrus Minor air-cooled engines, and it is pictured on a visit to Abingdon in September 1979.

Above: Developed from the early M.2 Hawk, the **Miles M.14 Magister** was a two-seat basic trainer powered by a 130hp de Havilland Gipsy Major engine. G-AJRS/P6382 is owned by the Shuttleworth Trust and is seen flying at Old Warden in July 1989.

Below: First flown in 1942, the **Miles M.38 Messenger** was used during its military career as a liaison aircraft. Production for the private owner continued post-war. G-AKIN is pictured at Cranfield in July 1987.

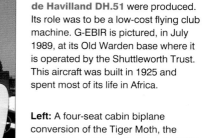

Above: Only three examples of the **de Havilland DH.51** were produced. Its role was to be a low-cost flying club machine. G-EBIR is pictured, in July 1989, at its Old Warden base where it is operated by the Shuttleworth Trust. This aircraft was built in 1925 and spent most of its life in Africa.

Left: A four-seat cabin biplane conversion of the Tiger Moth, the **Thruxton Jackaroo** first flew in 1957. The powerplant of a 130hp Gipsy Major remained unchanged, giving the type a less than sparkling performance. G-AOIR is seen at Cranfield in July 1987.

Left: First of the famous de Havilland 'Moth' range was the **DH.60 Moth**. It first flew in 1925 and had engines from 60 to 105hp. G-EBLV is pictured, in July 1989, flying over Hatfield, home of the company.

Below left: Featuring an enclosed cabin, the **de Havilland DH.80A Puss Moth** saw almost half its production go for export. G-ABLS is seen on the move at Hatfield in July 1987.

Below right: The most famous of all the 'Moths' is the **de Havilland DH.82 Tiger Moth**. Thousands of pilots learned their trade on this type. Australian-built G-AGZZ is pictured about to take off from Hatfield in July 1987.

Above left: With the pilot in an open cockpit, the **de Havilland DH.83 Fox Moth** had a cabin for four passengers. The type first flew in 1932, and was produced both in the UK and Canada: where G-AOJH, a DH.83C, originated. It has an enclosed cockpit to give some protection against the cold winters there. It is pictured at Hatfield in July 1987.

Above right: A follow-on design from the Puss Moth, the **de Havilland DH.85 Leopard Moth** was a full three-seater touring aircraft powered by a 130hp Gipsy Major. G-ATFU is seen at Cranfield, in July 1982. It has since been sold in New Zealand.

Right: Designed for the 1934 England to Australia air race, the **de Havilland DH.88 Comet** won the event ahead of a KLM DC-2. The winning aircraft was G-ACSS, which is now owned by the Shuttleworth Trust and is seen flying at Hatfield in July 1987.

Index of Preserved Aircraft

AEG G.IV 131
Aero Commander U-4B 100
Aero
  L-29 Delfin 48
  L-39 Albatros 12
Aero Spacelines Guppy 101
Aeronca C-3 147
AESL CT-4 Airtrainer 139
Aichi D3A 57
Airspeed Oxford 117
Albatros D.V 129
Alon Aircoupe 153
Antonov
  An-8 88
  An-10 88
  An-12 88
  An-14 9
  An-22 89
  An-24 89
  An-26 91
Arado
  Ar 196 58
  Ar 234 Blitz 58
Armstrong-Whitworth
  Argosy 114
Auster
  AOP.5 139
  J/5F Aiglet Trainer 148
Aviatik D1 127
Avro
  504K 129
  707 33
  Anson 116
  Avian 153
  Lancaster 76
  Lincoln 113
  Shackleton 95
  Tutor 145
  Vulcan 35
Avro Canada CF-100 29

BA Swallow II 154
BAC
  1-11 113
  167 Strikemaster 38
  221 33
  Concorde 113
  TSR.2 34
Bacon Super T-6 138
BAe AV-8A 25
Beech
  17 151
  18 108
  A65 Queen Air 94
  AT-11 Kansan 108
  Musketeer 133
  T-34 Mentor 139
Bell
  212 126
  47G 124
  AH-1G Cobra 124
  CH-136 Kiowa 120
  P-39 Airacobra 64
  P-59 Airacomet 22
  P-63 Kingcobra 64
  UH-1 Iroquois 126
  X-1 23
  YAH-63 120
Bellanca CH-300 153
Beriev
  Be-6 87
  Be-12 88
  Be-30 88
Blackburn
  B2 152
  Beverley 109
  Buccaneer 40
Boeing
  100E 144
  247 97
  307 Stratoliner 98
  367-80 101
  720 102
  727-22C 118
  747 98

B-17 Flying Fortress 61, 62
B-29 Superfortress 78, 79
B-47 Stratojet 27
B-50 96
B-52 Stratofortress 26, 27
C-97 Stratofreighter 100, 101
C-135/KC-135 101, 102
FB-5 143
P-26 144
PT-17 Stearman 136
YC-14 104
YL-15 134
Boeing-Vertol
  CH-113 Labrador 119
  YUH-61 121
  XCH-62 123
Boulton Paul
  Defiant 74
  P.IIIA 32
  Sea Balliol T.21 138
Breguet BR.273 128
Bristol
  188 32
  Beaufighter 71
  Blenheim 74
  Britannia 114, 115
  Bulldog 144
  F2b Fighter 130
  Freighter 114
  Sycamore 119
Bücker
  Bü 131B Jungmann 149
  Bü 133C Jungmeister 149

Canadair
  C-4 North Star 106
  CF-5 5
  CL-13 Sabre 14, 15
  CL-215 106
  CL-28 Argus 108
  CL-41 Tutor 4
CASA
  2-111 75
  207 Azor 107
  212 Aviocar 104
  352 85
Caudron
  C366 143
  G.3 131
Cavalier Mustang Mk.2 84
CCF Burnelli
  CBY-3 Loadmaster 87
Cessna
  O-1 Bird Dog 139
  150 138
  185/U-17 139
  195 148
  310 98
  A-37/T-37 3, 4
  O-2A 132
  T-50 Bobcat 99
  YH-41 123
Chrislea CH.3 Super Ace 151
Cierva C.8L 119
Commonwealth
  CA-12 Boomerang 60
  CA-16 Wirraway 135
  CA-18 83
  CA-25 Winjeel 139
Comper CLA 7 Swift 152
Consolidated
  B-24 Liberator 79
  PB2Y Coronado 98
  PB4Y Privateer 79
  PBY Catalina 61
Convair
  990 94
  B-36 94
  B-58 Hustler 27
  CV-240 99, 100
  CV-340 100
  F-102 Delta Dagger 7
  F-106 Delta Dart 9
  L-13 153
  Sea Dart 25

Curtiss
  68 Hawk III 140
  75 Hawk 141
  C-46 Commando 104, 105
  CW-15 Sedan 155
  F7C-1 Seahawk 141
  F9C-2 Sparrowhawk 141
  JN-4 Jenny 155
  NC4 143
  O-52 Owl 141
  P-40 64
  Robin 155
  SB2C Helldiver 74
  SNC-1 Falcon 141
  Wright Travel Air 152
Custer CCW-5 107

Dart G 150
Dassault
  MD.315 Flamant 86
  MD450 Ouragan 31
  Mirage III 31
  Mystère 20 85
  Mystère IVA 31
de Havilland
  DH.9 131
  DH.51 158
  DH.60 Moth 158
  DH.80A Puss Moth 158
  DH.82 Tiger Moth 158
  DH.83 Fox Moth 158
  DH.84 Dragon 118
  DH.85 Leopard Moth 158
  DH.88 Comet 158
  DH.89 Dragon Rapide 118
  DH.90 Dragonfly 118
  DH.98 Mosquito 81, 82
  DH.100 Vampire 41, 42
  DH.104 Dove 117
  DH.106 Comet 116, 117
  DH.110 Sea Vixen 36
  DH.112 Venom 42, 43
  DH.121 Trident 115
de Havilland Australia
  DHA-3 Drover 117
de Havilland Canada
  DHC-1 Chipmunk 136
  DHC-2 Beaver 132
  DHC-3 Otter 97
  DHC-4 Caribou 108
  DHC-5 Buffalo 94
  DHC-6 Twin Otter 105
Dewoitine
  D27 146
  D.520 77
DINFIA I.A.35 Huanquero 106
Dornier
  Do 24T 58
  Do 27 132
Douglas
  A-1 Skyraider 135
  A-20 Havoc 64
  A-26/B-26 Invader 80
  A3D Skywarrior 24
  A-4 Skyhawk 23
  B-18 Bolo 105
  B-23 Dragon 105
  B-66 Destroyer 24
  C-118 102
  C-124 100
  C-133 Cargomaster 94
  D-558-2 Skyrocket 23
  DB-7 Boston III 80
  DB8A-3P 142
  DC-3/C-47/R4D 110, 111, 112
  DC-4 Skymaster 105
  DC-6 102
  DC-7C 104
  DC-8-32 94
  F3D Skyknight 19
  F4D-1 Skyray 18
  F-5D Skylancer 18
  F-6A Skyray 18
  M-2 155
  O-38 142

O-46A 142
SBD Dauntless 64

EKW
  C-3603 134
  N20 Aiguillon 28
Embraer
  EMB-110 Bandeirante 99
English Electric
  Canberra 37
  Lightning 39
  P.1A 39
  Wren 153

Fabrica de Aviones
  I.Ae.27 Pulqui 34
Fairchild 24 157
  82D 144
  C-119 99
  C-123 Provider 106, 107
  Cornell 156
  FH-227D 97
  PT-23 138
Fairey
  Battle 77
  Delta II 33
  Firefly 75
  Fulmar 78
  Gannet 134
  Swordfish 72
Faucett F-19 97
FFA P.16 41
Fiat
  CR.32 143
  G91PAN 29
Fleet
  10/16 150
  21M 149
Fleetwing Seabird 148
FMA IA-58 Pucará 87
Focke-Wulf
  Fw 44J Stieglitz 151
  Fw 190 74, 75
Fokker
  D.VII 128
  D.XXI 78
  F.VIIa/3M 87
  S.11 Instructor 137
Folland Gnat 36
Ford Tri-Motor 103
Fouga Magister 1, 31

General Dynamics
  F-111 26
  F-16 8
Gloster
  E28/39 32
  Gauntlet 145
  Gladiator 145
  Javelin 36
  Meteor 40, 41
Gourdou-Leseurre GL22 145
Grumman
  AF Guardian 134
  A-6 Intruder 22
  C-1A Trader 103
  E-1B Tracer 103
  F3F-2 141
  F4F Wildcat 62
  F6F Hellcat 63
  F7F Tigercat 60
  F8F Bearcat 63
  F9F Cougar 21
  F9F Panther 20
  F11F Tiger 19
  F-14 Tomcat 25
  G-21 Goose 98
  G-22 Gulfhawk II 142
  HU-16 Albatross 106
  J2F Duck 142
  J4F-1 Widgeon 102
  OV-1 Mohawk 94
  S-2 Tracker 103
  TBM Avenger 58, 59

Halberstadt C.V 131
Handley Page
  Gugnunc 147
  Halifax 60, 61
  Hampden 78
  Hastings 115
  HP.115 32
  Jetstream 200 99
  Victor 35
  HPR.7 Herald 112
Hanriot HD.1 130
Harbin
  H-5 30
  Y-11 86
  Z5 122
Harlow PJC-2 148
Hawker
  Demon 1 145
  Hart Trainer 145
  Hind 145
  Hunter 38, 39
  Hurricane 65
  Kestrel 25
  P.1127 33
  Sea Fury 134, 135
  Sea Hawk 35
  Sea Hurricane 65
  Tempest 76
Hawker Siddeley
  748 112
  Andover E.3A 102
Heinkel
  He 111E 75
  He 162 57
Helio U-10A Super Courier 133
HFB 320 Hansa 86
Hispano
  HA-1112 Buchon 71
  HA-200 Saeta 29
Howard DGA-15 146
Hughes
  H-4 Hercules 100
  OH-6 Cayuse 124
Hunting
  H.126 32
  Jet Provost 37
Hurel-Dubois HD34 85

I.V.L. A22 Hansa 127
Ilyushin
  DB-3 52
  IL-2 54
  IL-10 54
  IL-12 89
  IL-14 89, 90
  IL-18 90
  IL-28 50
  IL-62 90
  IL-86 91

Junkers
  J9/D1 127
  Ju 52/1M 86
  Ju 52/3M 85
  Ju 87 58
  Ju 88 58
  W33 146
  W34 146

Kaman
  HH-43 Huskie 124
  SH-2 Seasprite 120
Kamov
  Ka-25 122
  Ka-26 123
Kawanishi
  N1K1 Kyofu 55
  N1K2-J Shiden Kai 55
Kawasaki
  Ki-48 56
  Ki-61 Hien 55
  Ki-100 56
Kochyerigin DI-6 52
Kreutzer K5 Air Coach 151

Latécoère **25** 144
Lavochkin
  La-7 53
  La-9 53
  La-11 53
  La-15 46
  La-250 46
Learfan 2100 95
Learjet 25 95
Lisunov **Li-2** 91
Lockheed
  12 Electra Junior 104
  A-12MD 24
  C-130 Hercules 100
  C-60 Lodestar 96
  Constellation 109, 110
  F-80/P-80 10
  F-94 Starfire 15, 16
  F-104 Starfighter 2, 7, 8
  AH-56 Cheyenne 118
  JetStar 96
  P2V Neptune 107, 108
  P-3 Orion 97
  P-38 Lightning 77
  PV2 Harpoon 96
  SR-71 24
  T2V-1 Seastar 3
  T-33 4, 5
  U-2 26
  Vega 150
  XFV-1 132
  XH-51A 121
  YO-3A 133
Loening OA-1A 142
LTV-Ryan-Hiller XC-142A 98
Luscombe 8A Silvaire 150
LVG C.VI 130

Macchi
  C202 Folgore 59
  Telegrafo No 1 130
Martin
  4-0-4 97
  AM-1 Mauler 134
  B-26 Marauder 81
  B-57 28
  PBM Marine 97
  SP-5 Marlin 101
Martinsyde F4 Buzzard 127
McCulloch YH-30 119
McDonnell
  220 95
  F-101 Voodoo 6, 7
  F2H-2 Banshee 16
  F3H Demon 22
  Phantom I 16
McDonnell Douglas
  F-15 Eagle 24
  F-4 Phantom II 17, 18
Messerschmitt
  Bf 108 Taifun 146
  Bf 109 71
  Bf 110 57
  Me 163B Komet 57
  Me 262 57
  Me 410 58
Mignet HM.14 Pou-de-Ciel 147
Mikoyan
  MiG-9 43
  MiG-15 45
  MiG-17 45
  MiG-21 44, 45
  MiG-23UB 43
  MiG-25 43, 44

MiG-27 43
MiG-29 43
MiG-31 44
Ye-166 44
Lim-5P 46
Mil
  Mi-2 123
  Mi-4 122
  Mi-6 121
  Mi-8 124
  Mi-10 121
  Mi-14PL 127
  Mi-24 123
  Mi-25E 123
  V-12 122
Miles
  M.2R Hawk Major 157
  M.14 Magister 157
  M.38 Messenger 157
  M.65 Gemini 157
Mitsubishi
  A6M Reisen 55
  J2M Raiden 56
  J8M1 Shusui 54
  Ki-46 56
  MU-2 104
Monocoupe 110 152
Morane-Saulnier
  MS.147 149
  MS.500 60
  MS.760 Paris 36
Myasishchev
  M-4 51
  M-17 51
  M-50 50

Nakajima
  B5N 57
  J1N1-S Gekko 55
  Ki-43 Hayabusa 55
  Kikka 55
NAMC YS-11 93
Nanchang
  CJ-6 136
  J-12 30
  Q-5 30
Naval Aircraft Factory N3N-3 151
Neiva N.621 Universal (T-25) 148
New Standard D25 154
Nieuport
  17C 129
  28C Bébé 128
Nieuport-Delage 29C 129
Noorduyn Norseman 147
Nord
  2501 Noratlas 86
  N1500 Griffon 31
North American
  A-5 Vigilante 21
  AJ Savage 101
  B-25 Mitchell 80, 81
  B-45 Tornado 26
  FJ Fury 16
  F-82 Twin Mustang 60
  F-86 Sabre 12, 13, 14
  F-100 Super Sabre 5, 6
  F-107 9
  L-17 Navion 151
  NA-50 154
  NA-64/BT-9 Yale 66
  O-47B 143
  P-51 Mustang 82, 83, 84
  T-28 Trojan 140
  T-39 Sabreliner 96

T-6 Harvard/Texan 66, 67
XB-70 Valkyrie 26
Northrop
  A-9 19
  Alpha 149
  C-125 Raider 93
  F-5 25
  F-20 25
  F-89 Scorpion 15
  P-61 Black Widow 73
  T-38A Talon 3
  YF-17 5
  YF-23 25

Pasped Skylark 151
Peking/Beijing NR1 87
Percival
  P.6 Mew Gull 147
  P.54 Prince 117
  Prentice 137
  Proctor 147
  Provost T.1 139
Petlyakov Pe-2 53
Pfalz D.XII 128
Piasecki
  H-25 Retriever 120
  HUP-3 120
Pilatus P.2 136
Piper PA-18 Super Cub 154
Pitcairn PCA-2 Autogiro 119
Polikarpov
  I-15 52
  I-16 52
  Po-2 150
Pyorremyrsky PM1 78
PZL
  M15 Belphegor 87
  PZL-104 Wilga 137
  TS-11 Iskra 48

Reid & Sigrist RS4 Desford 154
Republic
  A-10 19
  F-84 series 10, 11, 12
  F-91 15
  F-105 Thunderchief 8, 9
  P-47 Thunderbolt 70
Rockwell OV-10 Bronco 95
Royal Aircraft Factory
  BE2C 131
  RE8 128
  SE5a 130
RTAF 5 132
Ryan
  FR-1 Fireball 133
  G2-W Flamingo 155
  NYP 156
  PT-22 156
  STM 153

Saab
  91 Safir 137
  J29 29
  J32 Lansen 28
  J35 Draken 28
  J37 Viggen 29
Saro SRA.1 34
Saunders-Roe
  Skeeter 119
  SR.53 33
Scottish Aviation
  Pioneer 133
  Twin Pioneer 115
Shavrov Sh-1 155

Shenyang
  J-5 30
  J-6 30
  J-8 30
Short
  Belfast 115
  Sandringham 113
  SC.1 33
  Solent 114
SIAI-Marchetti SF.260 137
Sikorsky
  H-5 125
  H-19 Chickasaw 126
  H-34 125
  CH-37B 121
  HH-52 Seaguard 124
  CH-54 Tarhe 122
  Hoverfly 121
  VS-300 120
  VS-44A 95
  YR-5A 124
Soko
  J-20 Kraguj 133
  Type 522 138
Sopwith
  Camel 127
  Pup 129
  Snipe 131
  1½ Strutter 129
SPAD
  13 C.1 130
  S.7 130
Stampe SV.4 148
Stinson
  105 Voyager 156
  Reliant 156
  SM-1 Detroiter 156
Sud
  Alouette III 121
  SE-210 Caravelle 85
Sud-Ouest
  SO 4050 Vautour 31
Sukhoi
  Su-2 53
  Su-7 48
  Su-9 48
  Su-11 49
  Su-15UT 49
  Su-17M-3 49
  Su-20 49
  Su-22M-4 49
  Su-24 50
  Su-25 49
  Su-27 50
  T-4 50
  T-58D-2 49
  T-6-1 49
Supermarine
  510 32
  Attacker 34
  Scimitar 34
  Seagull V 73
  Spitfire 67, 68, 69
  Stranraer 143
  Swift 37
  Walrus 73
Tachikawa
  Ki-36 56
  Ki-55 56
Taylor Aerocar I 154
Thomas-Morse S4C 128
Thruxton Jackaroo 157
Tipsy B 148

Tupolev
  SB-2 53
  Tu-2 54
  Tu-4 93
  Tu-16 51, 52
  Tu-22 51
  Tu-95 87
  Tu-104 92
  Tu-114 92
  Tu-124 92
  Tu-128 52
  Tu-134 92
  Tu-144 93
  Tu-154 92
Turner RT-14 Meteor 149

Valtion Humu 77
Vertol
  44 125
  H-21 Shawnee 125
Vickers
  Valiant 35
  Varsity 116
  VC-10 113
  Viking 116
  Vimy 128
  Viscount 117
  Wellington 78
Voisin LA5-B2 127
Vought
  A-7 Corsair II 22
  F4U Corsair 72, 73
  F7U Cutlass 18
  F-8 Crusader 19, 20
  OS2U Kingfisher 70
  V93S Corsair 142
Vultee
  BT-13 Valiant 138
  L-1 Vigilant 154
  V-1A 150

Waco UPF-7 154
Westland
  (Bristol) Belvedere 118
  Lysander 73
  Wasp 118
  Wessex 60 126
  Wyvern 133

Xian
  F-7 29
  Y-7 89

Yakovlev
  Yak-3 59
  Yak-7UTI 78
  Yak-9 59
  Yak-11 140
  Yak-15 47
  Yak-17 47
  Yak-18 136
  Yak-23 47
  Yak-24 122
  Yak-25 46, 47
  Yak-27R 47
  Yak-28R 47
  Yak-36 46
  Yak-38 46
  Yak-38M 46
  Yak-40 91
  Yak-42 91
  Yak UT-1/Air-14 152
  Yak UT-2 152
Yun-5 88

Zlin 226 Trener 137

Bibliography

Aircraft Museums and Collections of the World (various editions):
Bob Ogden; Bob Ogden Publications

Aircraft of the Royal Air Force since 1918: Owen Thetford; Putnam

British Naval Aircraft since 1912: Owen Thetford; Putnam

The Encyclopaedia of Russian Aircraft, 1875-1995: Bill Gunston; Osprey

German Aircraft of the Second World War: J R Smith & Antony Kay; Putnam

United States Military Aircraft since 1909: G Swanborough & P M Bowers; Putnam

United States Naval Aircraft since 1911: G Swanborough & P M Bowers; Putnam

US Army Aircraft since 1947: Stephen Harding; Airlife.

Wrecks & Relics (various editions): Ken Ellis; Midland Publishing